STYLE GUIDE

STYLE GUIDE

THE ECONOMIST IN ASSOCIATION WITH
PROFILE BOOKS LTD

Published by Profile Books Ltd,
58A Hatton Garden, London ECIN 8LX

The greatest care has been taken in compiling this book.
However, no responsibility can be accepted by the publishers or compilers
for the accuracy of the information presented.

Printed in Great Britain by St Edmundsbury Press

A CIP catalogue record for this book is available
from the British Library

ISBN 1 86197 209 1

Contents

Preface

Every newspaper has its own style book, a set of rules telling journalists whether to write Peking or Beijing, Gadaffi or Qaddafi, judgement or judgment. *The Economist's* style book does this and a bit more. It also warns writers of some common mistakes and encourages them to write with more clarity and simplicity.

To make the style guide of wider general interest, additional mater-ial has been added, drawing on the series of reference books published under The Economist Books imprint.

All the prescriptive judgments in this style guide, however, are directly derived from those used each week in writing and editing *The Economist*.

Throughout the text, bold type is used to indicate examples. Words in SMALL CAPITALS indicate a separate but relevant entry (except in the paragraphs headed ABBREVIATIONS, where the use of small capitals is discussed).

This new, updated and revised edition of *The Economist Style Guide* is in three sections. The first is based on the style book used by those who edit *The Economist*; it is largely the work of John Grimond, the foreign editor. The second, on American and British English, describes the main differences between the two great English-speaking areas, in spelling, grammar and usage. The third part gathers together in one place lots of useful reference material.

Introduction

O N only two scores can *The Economist* hope to outdo its rivals consistently. One is the quality of its analysis; the other is the quality of its writing. The aim of this style guide is to give general advice on writing, to point out some common errors and to set some arbitrary rules.

The first requirement of *The Economist* is that it should be readily understandable. Clarity of writing usually follows clarity of thought. So think what you want to say, then say it as simply as possible. Keep in mind George Orwell's six elementary rules ("Politics and the English Language", 1946):

1. Never use a METAPHOR, simile or other figure of speech which you are used to seeing in print.
2. Never use a long word where a SHORT WORD will do.
3. If it is possible to cut out a word, always cut it out.
4. Never use the passive where you can use the ACTIVE.
5. Never use a FOREIGN PHRASE, a scientific word or a JARGON word if you can think of an everyday English equivalent.
6. Break any of these rules sooner than say anything outright barbarous.

Readers are primarily interested in what you have to say. By the way in which you say it you may encourage them either to read on or to stop reading. If you want them to read on:

1. Do not be stuffy. "To write a genuine, familiar or truly English style", said Hazlitt, "is to write as anyone would speak in common conversation who had a thorough command or choice of words or who could discourse with ease, force and perspicuity setting aside all pedantic and oratorical flourishes."

Use the language of everyday speech, not that of spokesmen, lawyers or bureaucrats (so prefer **let** to **permit, people** to **persons, buy** to **purchase, colleague** to **peer, way out** to **exit, present** to **gift, rich** to **wealthy, break** to **violate**). It is sometimes useful to talk of **human-rights abuses** but often the sentence can be rephrased more pithily and more accurately. **The army is accused of committing numerous human-rights abuses** probably means **The army is accused of torture and murder.**

Avoid, where possible, euphemisms and circumlocutions promoted by interest-groups. The **hearing-impaired** are simply **deaf.** It is no disrespect to the **disabled** sometimes to describe them as **crippled. Female teenagers** are **girls**, not **women**. The **underprivileged** may be **disadvantaged**, but are more likely just **poor**.

And **man** sometimes includes **woman**, just as **he** sometimes makes do for **she** as well. So long as you are not insensitive in other ways, few women will be offended if you do not use **or she** after every he.

> He or she which hath no stomach to this fight,
> Let him or her depart; his or her passport shall be made,
> And crowns for convoy put into his or her purse:
> We would not die in that person's company
> That fears his or her fellowship to die with us.

2. Do not be hectoring or arrogant. Those who disagree with you are not necessarily stupid or insane. Nobody needs to be described as silly: let your analysis prove that he is. When you express opinions, do not simply make assertions. The aim is not just to tell readers what you think, but to persuade them; if you use arguments, reasoning and evidence, you may succeed. Go easy on the oughts and shoulds.

3. Do not be too pleased with yourself. Don't boast of your own cleverness by telling readers that you correctly predicted something or that you have a scoop. You are more likely to bore or irritate them than to impress them. So keep references to *The Economist* to a minimum, particularly those of the we-told-you-so variety. References to "this correspondent" or "your correspondent" are always self-conscious and they are often self-congratulatory.

4. Do not be too chatty. **Surprise, surprise** is more irritating than informative. So is **Ho, ho,** etc.

5. Do not be too didactic. A recent issue of *The Economist* had an imperative on six out of seven consecutive pages. If too many sentences begin **Compare, Consider, Expect, Imagine, Look at, Note, Prepare for, Remember** or **Take**, readers will think they are reading a textbook (or, indeed, a style book). This may not be the way to persuade them to renew their subscriptions.

6. Do not be sloppy in the construction of your sentences and paragraphs. Do not use a participle unless you make it clear what it applies to. Thus avoid **Having died, they had to bury him**, or **Proceeding along this line of thought, the cause of the train crash becomes clear.**
Don't overdo the use of **don't, isn't, can't, won't**, etc.

Use the subjunctive properly. If you are posing a hypothesis contrary to fact, you must use the subjunctive. Thus, **If Hitler were alive today, he could tell us whether he kept a diary.** If the hypothesis may or may not be true, you do not use the subjunctive: **If this diary is not Hitler's, we shall be glad we did not publish it.** If you have **would** in the main clause, you must use the subjunctive in the if clause. **If you were to disregard this rule, you would make a fool of yourself.**

In general, be concise. Try to be economical in your account or argument ("The best way to be boring is to leave nothing out" – Voltaire). Similarly, try to be economical with words.

Do your best to be lucid. Simple sentences help. Keep complicated constructions and gimmicks to a minimum, if necessary by remembering the *New Yorker*'s comment: "Backward ran sentences until reeled the mind." Mark Twain described how a good writer treats sentences: "At times he may indulge himself with a long one, but he will make sure there are no folds in it, no vaguenesses, no parenthetical interruptions of its view as a whole; when he has done with it, it won't be a sea-serpent with half of its arches under the water; it will be a torch-light procession."

Long paragraphs, like long sentences, can confuse the reader. "The paragraph," according to Fowler, "is essentially a unit of thought, not of length; it must be homogeneous in subject matter and sequential in treatment." One-sentence paragraphs should be used only occasionally.

Clear thinking is the key to clear writing. "A scrupulous writer," observed Orwell, "in every sentence that he writes will ask himself at least four questions, thus: What am I trying to say? What words will express it? What image or idiom will make it clearer? Is this image fresh enough to have an effect? And he will probably ask himself two more: Could I put it more shortly? Have I said anything that is avoidably ugly?"

Scrupulous writers will also notice that their copy is edited only lightly and is likely to be used. It may even be read.

3

A note on editing

Editing has always made a large contribution to *The Economist's* excellence. It should continue to do so. But editing on a screen is beguilingly simple. It is quite easy to rewrite an article without realising that one has done much to it at all: the cursor leaves no trace of crossings out, handwritten insertions, rearranged sentences or reordered paragraphs. The temptation is to continue to make changes until something emerges which the editor himself might have written. One benefit of this is a tightly edited newspaper. One cost is a certain sameness. The risk is that the newspaper will turn into a collection of 70 or 80 articles which read as though they have been written by no more than half a dozen hands. *The Economist* has a single editorial outlook, and it is anonymous. But it is the work of many people, both in London and abroad, as its datelines testify. If the prose of our Tokyo correspondent is indistinguishable from the prose of our Nairobi correspondent, readers will feel they are being robbed of variety. They may also wonder whether these two people really exist, or whether the entire newspaper is not written in London. The moral for editors is that they should respect good writing. That is mainly what this style guide is designed to promote. It is not intended to impose a single style on all *The Economist's* journalists. A writer's style, after all, should reflect his mind and personality. So long as they are compatible with *The Economist's*, and so long as the prose is good, editors should exercise suitable self-restraint. Remember that your copy, too, will be edited. And even if you think you are not guilty, bear in mind this comment from John Gross:

> Most writers I know have tales to tell of being mangled by editors and mauled by fact-checkers, and naturally it is the flagrant instances they choose to single out – absurdities, outright distortions of meaning, glaring errors. But most of the damage done is a good deal less spectacular. It consists of small changes (usually too boring to describe to anyone else) that flatten a writer's style, slow down his argument, neutralise his irony; that ruin the rhythm of a sentence or the balance of a paragraph; that deaden the tone that makes the music. I sometimes think of the process as one of "de-sophistication".

John Grimond

PART I

THE ESSENCE OF STYLE

A

ABBREVIATIONS. Unless an abbreviation or acronym is so familiar that it is used more often than the full form (eg, BBC, CIA, DNA, EU, FBI, IMF, NATO, OECD, WTO), write the words in full on first appearance: thus **Trades Union Congress** (not TUC). After the first mention, try not to repeat the abbreviation too often; so write **the agency** rather than **the** IAEA, **the Union** rather than **the** EU, to avoid spattering the page with capital letters. There is no need to give the initials of an organisation if it is not referred to again.

If an abbreviation can be pronounced (eg, EFTA, NATO, UNESCO), it does not generally require the definite article. Other organisations, except companies, should usually be preceded by the (**the** BBC, **the** NHS, **the** KGB, **the** UNCHR and **the** NIESR). Use MP only after first spelling out Member of Parliament in full (in many places an MP is a military policeman).

Those abbreviations that can be pronounced and are composed of bits of words rather than just initials should be spelled out in upper and lower case: **Cocom, Frelimo, Legco, Mercosur, Renamo, Unicef, Unison, Unprofor.** (See also INITIALS.) But write AIDS, UNITA.

In bodymatter, abbreviations, whether they can be pronounced as words or not (GNP, GDP, FOB, CIF, D-**marks**, T-**shirts**, X-**rays**), should be set in small capitals, with no points – unless they are currencies like **DM** or **FFr**, elements like **H** and **O** or degrees of temperature like °**F** and °**C**. Brackets, apostrophes (see PUNCTUATION) and all other typographical furniture accompanying small capitals are generally set in ordinary roman, with a lower-case s (also roman) for plurals and genitives. Thus IOUS, MPS' salaries, SDRS, etc. But ampersands are set as small capitals, as are numerals and any hyphens attaching them to a small capital. Thus R&D, A23, M1, F-16, etc. See also AMPERSANDS.

Abbreviations that include upper-case and lower-case letters must be set in a mixture of small capitals and lower case: BAe, BPhil, PhDs.

Use lower case for **kg, km, lb** (never **lbs**), **kph, mph** and other MEASURES, and for **ie, eg**, which should both be followed by commas. When used with figures, these lower-case abbreviations should follow immediately, with no space (**11am, 15kg, 35mm, 100mph, 78rpm**), as should AD and BC (AD76, 55BC), although they are set in small capitals. Two abbreviations together, however, must be separated: **60m b/d**.

Most scientific units, except those of temperature, that are named after individuals should be set in small capitals, though any attachments denoting multiples go in lower case. Thus **watt** is **w**, whereas **kilowatt, milliwatt** and **megawatt**, meaning 1,000 watts, one-thousandth of a watt and 1m watts, are abbreviated to kw, mw and mw.

The elements do not take small capitals. Lead is Pb, carbon dioxide is CO_2, methane is CH_4. Chlorofluorocarbons are, however, CFCs, and the oxides of nitrogen are generally NOX. Different isotopes of the same element are distinguished by raised prefixes: carbon-14 is ^{14}C, helium-3 is ^3He.

Most upper-case abbreviations take upper-case initial letters when written in full (eg, the LSO is the London Symphony Orchestra), but there are exceptions: CAP but common agricultural policy, EMU but economic and monetary union, GDP but gross domestic product, PSBR but public-sector borrowing requirement, VLSI but very large-scale integration.

Do not use Prof, Sen, Gen, Col, etc. But Lieut-Colonel and Lieut-Commander are permissible. So is Rev, but it must be preceded by the and followed by a Christian name or initial: the Rev Jesse Jackson (thereafter Mr Jackson). Always use chief executive rather than CEO.

Always spell out page, pages, hectares, miles. But kilograms (not kilogrammes) and kilometres can be shortened to kg (or kilos) and km.

Remember that the FAO is the Food and Agriculture Organisation, IDA is the International Development Association, NAFTA is the North American Free-Trade Agreement, the OAU is the Organisation of African Unity, the PLO is the Palestine Liberation Organisation.

Remember, too, that the v of HIV stands for virus, so do not write HIV virus.

Write Euro-MPs, not MEPs.

-ABLE, -EABLE, -IBLE. The following lists are not comprehensive.

-able

debatable	implacable	movable
dispensable	indescribable	tradable
disputable	indictable	unmistakable
forgivable	indispensable	unshakable
imaginable	indistinguishable	

-eable

likeable	rateable	traceable
manageable	serviceable	unpronounceable

-ible

accessible	inadmissible	irresistible
convertible	indestructible	permissible
digestible	investible	submersible

ACCENTS. On words now accepted as English, use accents only when they make a crucial difference to pronunciation: **cliché, soupçon, façade, café, communiqué** (but **elite, feted**). If you use one accent, use all: **émigré, mêlée, protégé, résumé.** See also ACCENTS, page 94.

Put the accents and cedillas on French names and words, umlauts on German ones and tildes (but not other accents) on Spanish ones: **Françoise de Panafieu, Wolfgang Schäuble, Federico Peña.** Leave the accents off names in other foreign languages.

Any foreign word in italics should, however, be given its proper accents.

ACRONYM: this is a word, like **radar** or NATO, not a set of initials, like the BBC or the IMF.

ACTIVE, NOT PASSIVE. Be direct. **A hit B** describes the event more concisely than **B was hit by A.**

ADVERBS. Put adverbs where you would put them in normal speech, which is usually after the verb. But see also AMERICANISMS and PART II.

AFFECT means to have an influence on, as in **The novel affected his attitude to immigrants.** See also EFFECT.

AFFINITY is by definition mutual. It can exist **between** or **with** things, but not **to** or **for** them.

AGGRAVATE means **make worse,** not **irritate** or **annoy.**

AGGRESSION is an unattractive quality, so do not call a **keen** salesman an aggressive one (unless his foot is in the door – or beyond).

AGONY COLUMN: when Sherlock Holmes perused this, it was a **personal column**, not letters to an **agony aunt**.

AGREE: things are agreed **on, to** or **about**, not just agreed.

ALIBI. An **alibi** is the proven fact of being elsewhere, not a false explanation.

ALTERNATE, as an adjective, means **every other.**

ALTERNATIVE: strictly, this is **one of two**, not one of three, four, five or more (which may be **options**).

AMEND is not quite the same as **emend**; though both result in an improvement, **emend** is used only of something written. **He amended his life by giving up gambling and drinking,** but **He emended his memo by correcting the spelling mistakes.**

AMERICANISMS. Use Americanisms discriminatingly. Many American words and expressions have passed into the language; others have vigour, particularly if used occasionally. Some are short and to the point (so prefer **lay off** to **make redundant**). But many are unnecessarily long (so use **and** not **additionally, car** not **automobile, company** not **corporation, transport** not **transportation, district** not **neighbourhood, oblige** not **obligate, stocks** not **inventories** unless there is the risk of confusion with stocks and shares).

Grow a beard or a tomato but not a company. By all means **call for** a record profit if you wish to exhort the workers, but not if you merely predict one. Do not **post** it if it has been achieved. If it has not, look for someone new to **head** the company, not to **head it up.**

Try not to verb nouns or to adjective them. So do not **access** files, **haemorrhage** red ink (**haemorrhage** is a noun), let one event **impact**

another, **author** books (still less **co-author** them), **critique** style sheets, **host** parties or **loan** money. **Gunned down** means **shot**.

Choose tenses according to British usage. In particular, do not fight shy of the perfect tense, especially where no date or time is given. Thus **Mr Clinton has woken up to the danger** is preferable to **Mr Clinton woke up to the danger,** unless you can add **last week** or **when he heard the explosion.**

Americans put the adverbs before the verb; the British put them after, as in normal speech. See also PART II.

AMONG is correct. Do not use **amongst.**

AMPERSANDS. Ampersands should be used as follows.
1. When they form part of the name of a company, like AT&T, **Pratt & Whitney.**
2. For such things as constituencies or other compound names where two names are linked to form one unit. (Eg, **The rest of Brighouse & Spenborough joined with the Batley part of Batley & Morley to form Batley & Spen.** Or **The area thus became the Pakistani province of Kashmir and the Indian state of Jammu & Kashmir.**)
3. In R&D, M&A and S&L.

AN should be used before any word beginning with a vowel sound (**an egg, an umbrella, an** MP) or an h if, and only if, the h is silent. So **a hospital, a hotel,** but **an honorary degree, a European university, a** U-turn.

ANARCHY means the **complete absence of law** or government. It may be harmonious or chaotic.

ANIMALS, PLANTS, ETC. When it is necessary to use a Latin name, follow the standard practice. Thus for all creatures higher than viruses, write the binomial name in italics, giving an initial capital to the first word (the genus): *Turdus turdus,* the song thrush; *Metasequoia glyptostroboides,* the dawn redwood.

ANTICIPATE does not mean **expect.** Jack and Jill expected to marry; if they anticipated marriage, only Jill might find herself expectant.

ANY ONE refers to a number; **anyone** to anybody.

ANY WAY refers to any manner; **anyway** means **nevertheless.**

APPEAL is intransitive nowadays (except in America), so **appeal against** decisions.

APPRAISE means **set a price on**. **Apprise** means **inform**.

AS OF (April 5th or April): prefer **on** (or **after**, or **since**) April 5th, **in** April.

AS TO: there is usually a more appropriate preposition.

AUTARCHY means **absolute sovereignty**, but **autarky** means **self-sufficiency**.

B

Bale: in the hayfield, yes, otherwise **bail, bail out.** But **bale out** of a boat.

Beg the question means neither **invite** (or **raise**) **the question** nor **evade the answer.** To **beg the question** is to base a conclusion upon an assumption that is as much in need of proof as the conclusion itself. **All governments should promote free trade because otherwise protectionism will increase. This begs the question.**

Biannual can mean **twice a year** or **once every two years.** Avoid.

Biennial also means **once in two years,** so is best avoided too.

Bicentennial: prefer **bicentenary** (as a noun).

Black. In the black means **in profit** in Britain, but **making losses** in some places. Always use **in profit.**

Both ... and. A preposition placed after both should be repeated after and. Thus, **both to right and to left;** but **to both right and left** is all right.

Apply the same rule to **either ... or ... , neither ... nor ...** and **not only ... but (also) ...**

Brokerage is what a stockbroking firm does, not what it is.

C

CANUTE'S exercise on the seashore was designed to persuade his courtiers of what he knew to be true but they doubted, that he was not omnipotent. Don't imply he was surprised to get his feet wet.

CAPITALS.

A balance has to be struck between so many capitals that the eyes dance and so few that the reader is diverted more by our style than by our substance. The general rule is to dignify with capital letters organisations and institutions, but not people. More exact rules are laid out below. Even these, however, leave some decisions to individual judgment. If in doubt use lower case unless it looks absurd. And remember that "a foolish consistency is the hobgoblin of little minds" (Emerson).

1. People. Use upper case for ranks and titles when written in conjunction with a name, but lower case when on their own. Thus, **President Clinton**, but the **president**; **Vice-President Gore**, but the **vice-president**; **Colonel Qaddafi** but the **colonel**; **Pope John Paul**, but the **pope**; **Queen Elizabeth**, but the **queen**.

Do not write **Prime Minister Blair** or **Defence Secretary Cohen**; they are the **prime minister, Mr Blair**, and the **defence secretary, Mr Cohen**. You may, however, write **Chancellor Schröder**.

All office holders when referred to merely by their office, not by their name, are lower case: the **chancellor of the exchequer**, the **foreign secretary**, the **prime minister**, the **speaker**, the **treasury secretary**, the **president of the United States**, the **chairman of British Airways**.

The only exceptions are: (a) a few titles that would look unduly peculiar without capitals, eg, **Black Rod, Master of the Rolls, Chancellor of the Duchy of Lancaster, Lord Privy Seal, Lord Chancellor**; (b) a few exalted people, such as the **Dalai Lama**, the **Aga Khan**. Also **God**. See also TITLES.

2. Organisations, ministries, departments, treaties, acts, etc, generally take upper case when their full name (or something pretty close to it, eg, **State Department**) is used. Thus, **European Commission, Forestry Commission, Arab League, Amnesty International, the Household Cavalry, Ministry of Agriculture, Department of Trade and Industry, Treasury, Metropolitan Police, High Court, Supreme Court, Court of Appeal, Senate, Central Committee, Politburo, Oxford Uni-

versity, the New York Stock Exchange (but the London stock exchange, since that is only its informal name), the Treaty of Rome, the Health and Safety at Work Act, etc.

So, too, the House of Commons, House of Lords, House of Representatives, St Paul's Cathedral (the cathedral), World Bank (the Bank), Bank of England (the Bank), Department of State (the department).

But organisations, committees, commissions, special groups, etc, that are either impermanent, ad hoc, local or relatively insignificant should be lower case. Thus: the subcommittee on journalists' rights of the National Executive Committee of the Labour Party, the international economic subcommittee of the Senate Foreign Relations Committee, the Oxford University bowls club, Market Blandings rural district council.

Use lower case for rough descriptions (the Glass-Steagall act, the safety act, the American health department, the French parliament as distinct from its National Assembly). If you are not sure whether the English translation of a foreign name is exact or not, assume it is rough and use lower case.

Parliament and Congress are upper case. But the opposition is lower case, even when used in the sense of her majesty's loyal opposition. The government, the administration and the cabinet are always lower case.

3. The full name of political parties is upper case, including the word party: Republican Party, Labour Party, Peasants' Party. Note that only people are Democrats, Christian Democrats, Liberal Democrats or Social Democrats; their parties, policies, committees, etc, are Democratic, Christian Democratic, Liberal Democratic or Social Democratic (although a committee may be Democrat-controlled).

When referring to a specific party, write Labour, the Republican nominee, a prominent Liberal, etc, but use lower case in looser references to liberals, conservatism, communists, etc. Tories, however, are upper case.

4. A political, economic or religious label formed from a proper name, eg, Gaullism, Paisleyite, Leninist, Napoleonic, Wilsonian, Jacobite, Luddite, Marxist, Hobbesian, Christian, Buddhism, Hindu, Maronite, Finlandisation, Thatcherism, should have a capital.

5. In finance and government there are some particular exceptions to the general rule of initial caps for full names, lower case for informal ones. Use caps for the World Bank and the Fed (after first spelling it

out as the **Federal Reserve**), although these are shortened, informal names. The **Bank of England** and its foreign equivalents have initial caps when named formally and separately, but collectively they are central banks in lower case (except Ireland's, which is actually named the **Central Bank**). **Special drawing rights** are lower case but abbreviated in small caps as SDRS, except when used with a figure as a currency (**SDR500m**). **Deutschmarks** are usually just D-**marks**. Treasury bonds issued by America's Treasury should be upper case; treasury bills (or bonds) of a general kind should be lower case. Avoid **T-bonds** and **t-bills.**

After first mention, the **House of Commons** (or **Lords**, or **Representatives**) becomes the **House**, the **World Bank** and **Bank of England** become the **Bank** and the IMF can become the **Fund**. Organisations with unusual names, such as the **African National Congress, Civic Forum** and the **European Union**, become the **Congress**, the **Forum** and the **Union**. But most other organisations, agencies, banks, commissions (including the **European Commission**), etc, take lower case when referred to incompletely on second mention.

6. Places. Use initial capitals for definite geographical places, regions, areas and countries (**The Hague, Transylvania, Germany**), and for vague but recognised political or geographical areas: the **Middle East, South Atlantic, East Asia** (which is to be preferred to the **Far East**), the **West** (as in the decline of the West), the **Gulf, North Atlantic, South-East Asia**, the **Midlands, Central America**, the **West Country, Western Europe, Eastern Europe, Central Europe.**

Use lower case for **east, west, north, south** except when part of a name (**North Korea, South Africa, West End**) or when part of a thinking group: the **South** (in the United States), the **Highlands** (of Scotland). But use lower case if you are, say, comparing regions of the United States, some of which are merely geographical areas: **House prices in the north-east and the south are rising faster than those in the mid-west and the south-west.**

Use **West Germany** (**Berlin**) and **East Germany** (**Berlin**) only in historical references. They are now **western Germany** (**western Berlin**) and **eastern Germany** (**eastern Berlin**).

The **third world** (an unsatisfactory term now that the communist second world has disappeared) is lower case.

If in doubt, use lower case (**the sunbelt**).

Use capitals for particular buildings, even if the name is not strictly accurate (eg, the **Foreign Office**).

Use lower case for province, river, state, city when not strictly part of the name: the **Limpopo river, Washington state, Cabanas** province, Guatemala city, Kuwait city, New York city, Panama city, Quebec city (but the River Thames, Mississippi River, Dodge City, Ho Chi Minh City, Kansas City, Oklahoma City, Salt Lake City).

7. Use capitals to avoid confusion, especially with no (and therefore yes). **In Bergen no votes predominated** suggests a stalemate, whereas **In Bergen No votes predominated** suggests a triumph of noes over yeses. In most contexts, though, yes and no should be lower case: "The answer is no."

8. Euro-terms
The usual rules apply for the full, proper names and their informal use. Thus:
European Commission, the **commission**
European Parliament, the **parliament**
Treaty of Rome, the **Rome treaty**
Treaty on European Union, the **Maastricht treaty**

But the **European Union** becomes the **Union** on subsequent mention.

Write **Eurobond, Euroyen bond, Euromarket, Europhile, Europhobe** and **Eurosceptic,** but **euro** (the currency) in body text. Other Euro-terms are hyphened. See also CURRENCIES.

9. The e-world

CD-ROM	e-business	the net
cyber-attack	e-commerce	online
cyber-soccer, etc	e-mail	the web
cybernetics	Internet	website
cyberspace	laptop	World Wide Web
cyberwars		

10. Others
Some political terms (upper case)

Communist (if a party)	Parliament	Teamster
Congress	Social Security	Tory
the Crown	(American)	

Historical periods (upper case)

Black Death	Renaissance
the Depression	Restoration
Middle Ages	Year of the Dog (but new year
New Deal	and new year's day)

Trade names (upper case)
Hoover, Teflon, Valium, Walkman, etc

Miscellaneous (upper case)

A-levels	Latinos
anti-Semitism	Mafia (the genuine article)
the Bar	Pershing missile
Catholics	Protestants
Cloudcuckooland	Pyrrhic
Coloureds (in South Africa)	Semitic (-ism)
the Cup Final	Stealth fighter, bomber, missile
the Davis Cup	Test match
Fund (as in imf)	Utopia (-n)
Hispanics	Wild West
House of Laity	Young Turks
the Koran	

Miscellaneous (lower case)

19th amendment	cruise missile	the pope
(but Article 19)	cultural revolution	the press
aborigines	french windows	the queen
administration	general synod	realpolitik
angst	government	the right
blacks	industrial revolution	the second world war
cabinet	Labour day	six-day war
Christmas day	the left	the speaker
civil servant	mafia (any old group	third world
civil service	of criminals)	state-of-the-union
cold war	mid-west	message
common market	new year	white paper
communist (generally)	new year's day	
constitution	opposition	

CARTEL. A cartel is a group that restricts supply in order to drive up prices. Do not use it to describe any old syndicate or association of producers.

CASE. "There is perhaps no single word so freely resorted to as a trouble-saver," says Gowers, "and consequently responsible for so much flabby writing." Often you can do without it. **There are many cases of it being unnecessary** is better as **It is often unnecessary. If it is the case that** ... simply means **If. It is not the case** means **It is not so.**

CASSANDRA'S predictions were correct but not believed.

CATALYST. This is something that speeds up a chemical reaction while itself remaining unchanged. Do not confuse it with one of the agents.

CENSOR. The critics may **censure** a bad play, but oppose any attempt to **censor** it, that is **suppress all or part** of it.

CENTRED on, not **around** or **in.**

CHARGE. If you **charge** intransitively, do so as a bull, cavalry officer or some such, not as an **accuser** (so avoid **The standard of writing was abysmal, he charged**).

CIRCUMSTANCES stand **around** a thing, so it is **in,** not **under,** them.

COLLAPSE is not a transitive verb. You may collapse, but you may not collapse something.

COLLECTIVE NOUNS. There is no firm rule about the number of a verb governed by a singular collective noun. It is best to go by the sense, ie, whether the collective noun stands for a single entity (**The council was elected in March, The me generation has run its course, The staff is loyal**) or for its constituents (**The council are at sixes and sevens over taxes, The preceding generation are all dead, The staff are at each other's throats**).

A rule for **number: The number is ... , A number are ...**

A pair and **a couple** are both plural.

A rule for **majority:** when it is used in an abstract sense, it takes the singular; when it is used to denote the elements making up the majority, it should be plural. **A two-thirds majority is needed to amend the constitution** but **A majority of the Senate were opposed.**

A **government,** a **party,** a **company** (whether Tesco or Marks and Spencer) and a **partnership** (Skidmore, Owings & Merrill) are all **it,** and take a singular verb. So does a **country,** even if its name looks plural. Thus **The United States is helping the Philippines.** The **United Nations** is singular. **Politics** is also singular; so are **economics, mechanics, physics** and **statics** – though not **antics, hysterics, tactics** or **statistics.**

Brokers too. **Legg Mason Wood Walk is preparing a statement.** Avoid **stockbrokers Furman Selz Mager, bankers Chase Manhattan** or **accountants Ernst & Young.** And remember that **Barclays** is a **British bank,** not **the British bank,** just as **Ford** is **a car company,** not **the car company** and **Luciano Pavarotti** is **an opera singer**, not **the opera singer**.

Some nouns ending in **s** are always treated as singular; they include **news** and games such as **darts, bowls** and **billiards**.

Law and order defies the rules of grammar and is singular.

COME UP WITH: try **suggest, originate** or **produce.**

COMPANIES.
Call companies by the names they call themselves.

Airbus Industrie
Aérospatiale
Allied Domecq
American Telephone and
  Telegraph (AT&T)
Anglo American
Banc One
B.A.T Industries
Bayerische Hypotheken- und
  Wechsel-Bank (space before
  the und, no hyphen after)
Benetton
Bertelsmann
Bloomingdale's
Boots (the chemist)
British Aerospace (BAe)
BSkyB
Cadbury Schweppes
Coca-Cola
Compaq
Conoco
ConsGold
Cummins Engine
Daimler-Chrysler
Donaldson, Lufkin & Jenrette
Dresdner Kleinwort Benson
DuPont
Eastman Kodak
Ericsson
Ernst & Young
Friedrich Krupp
Glaxo Wellcome

Goldman Sachs
Harrods
Hewlett-Packard
Hoare Govett
Hoechst
Hongkong & Shanghai Bank
  (but more likely HSBC Holdings)
Kohlberg Kravis Roberts
Kraft Foods
Lloyd's (insurance market)
Lloyds TSB (the bank)
Lord & Taylor
McDonald's
McDonnell Douglas
Marks and Spencer plc (but
  Marks & Spencer is the
  name above the shop)
E. Merck
Merrell
Merrill Lynch
Messerschmitt-Bölkow-Blohm
  (MBB)
Moët & Chandon
Moody's
J.P. Morgan
Motoren Turbine Union (MTU)
Novell
Nippon Telegraph and
  Telephone (NTT)
Pfizer
Philips
Pillsbury

19

PolyGram
Pratt & Whitney
PricewaterhouseCoopers
Procter & Gamble
Rolls-Royce (cars and aero
 engines)
Saks Fifth Avenue
Seagram
Sears, Roebuck

Shearson Lehman Hutton
SmithKline Beecham
Smith New Court
Standard & Poor's
Thyssen
Time Warner
Unix
Wal-Mart
Zeneca

Some other British and American company names are listed under STOCKMARKET INDICES (see pages 146–148ff).

COMPARE. A is compared **with** B when you draw attention to the difference. A is compared **to** B when you want to stress their similarity ("Shall I compare thee to a summer's day?")

COMPLAISANT people aim to please others; if they are **complacent**, they are pleased with themselves.

COMPOUND does not mean **make worse**. It may mean **combine** or, intransitively, **agree** or **come to terms**. To **compound a felony** means to **agree for a consideration not to prosecute**.

COMPRISE means **is composed of**. The Democratic coalition comprises women, workers, blacks and Jews. Women make up (not comprise) three-fifths of the Democratic coalition. Alternatively, Three-fifths of the Democratic coalition is composed of women.

CONTINUOUS describes something uninterrupted; **continual** admits of a break. If your neighbours play loud music every night, it is a **continual nuisance**; but it isn't a **continuous nuisance** unless the music is never turned off.

CONVINCE. Don't **convince** people to do something. In that context the word you want is **persuade**. The prime minister was persuaded to call a June election; he was convinced of the wisdom of doing so only after he had won.

COUNTRIES AND THEIR INHABITANTS. In most contexts sacrifice precision to simplicity and use **Britain** rather than **Great Britain** or the **United Kingdom**, and **America** rather than the **United States of America**. ("In all pointed sentences some degree of accuracy must be sacrificed to conciseness." Dr Johnson.) See also pages 140ff.

It is sometimes important to be precise in other contexts. Remember therefore that **Great Britain** consists of **England, Scotland** and **Wales**, which together with **Northern Ireland** (which we generally call **Ulster**, though Ulster strictly includes three counties in the republic of Ireland) make up the **United Kingdom**.

Ireland is simply **Ireland**. Although it is a republic, it is not the Republic of Ireland. Neither is it, in English, Eire.

Holland, though a nice, short, familiar name, is strictly only two of the 12 provinces that make up **the Netherlands**, and the **Dutch** are increasingly indignant about misuse of the shorter name. So use **the Netherlands**.

The primary definition of **Scandinavia** is Norway and Sweden, but it is often used to include Denmark, Iceland, Norway and Sweden, which, with Finland, make up the **Nordic countries**.

Where countries have made it clear that they wish to be called by a new (or an old) name, respect their requests. Thus **Côte d'Ivoire, Myanmar, Burkina Faso, Sri Lanka, Thailand, Zimbabwe, Congo**. See also PLACES, pages 49–50.

The former **Soviet Union** used often to be called **Russia**, particularly in foreign-policy contexts. But Russia today is the largest and most important of the countries that make up the COMMONWEALTH OF INDE-PENDENT STATES, which has 12 members, including Belarus (not Belorussia), Kazakhstan, Kirgizstan (not Kirgizia or Kyrgyzstan), Moldova (not Moldavia), Tajikistan, Turkmenistan (not Turkmenia) and Uzbekistan (see page 133).

Remember, too, that although it is usually all right to talk about the inhabitants of the United States as **Americans**, the term also applies to everyone from Canada to Cape Horn. It may sometimes be necessary to write **United States citizens**. Do not, however, use **US**, except where it is part of a company's name. In all cases it is best to refer to the specific nationality: thus **Canadians** rather than **North Americans**.

CREDIBLE means to **be believable; credulous** means **too ready to believe. Her explanation for missing the meeting was credible. His explanation that he found the money at the end of the rainbow convinced only the credulous.**

CRESCENDO. This is not an acme, apogee, peak, summit or zenith but a **passage of increasing loudness.** You cannot therefore **build to a crescendo.**

CRISIS. This is a decisive event or turning-point. Many of the economic and political troubles wrongly described as **crises** are really **persistent difficulties, sagas** or **affairs.**

CRITIQUE is a noun. If you want a verb, try **criticise.**

CURRENCIES. Use $ as the standard currency and in general convert currencies to $ on first mention. See also CURRENCIES, pages 105–110; FIGURES, pages 27–28; MEASUREMENTS, page 40; and MEASURES, pages 121ff.

Britain
1p, 2p, 3p, to 99p (*not* £0.99)   £5m–6m (*not* £5m–£6m)
£6 (*not* £6.00)   **£5 billion–6 billion**
£5,000–6000 (*not* £5,000–£6,000)   (*not* £5–6 billion)

America
$ will do generally. Spell out **cents.**

A$, C$, HK$, M$, NT$, NZ$ and **S$** are Australian, Canadian, Hong Kong, Malaysian, New Taiwan, New Zealand and Singapore $ (dollars). Other currencies include **DM, BFr, FFr, SFr, IR£** (punts), **ASch, Pta, SDR, DKr** (Danish krone, kroner), **NKr** (Norwegian krone, kroner), **SKr** (Swedish krona, kronor) and **¥.** With all these, write the abbreviation followed by the figure: **¥100** (not 100 yen), **Pta100** (not 100 pesetas), **SDR1m** (not 1m SDRS).

Sums in other currencies, including the **euro,** which will replace some of the currencies mentioned earlier, are written in full, with the number first: **100m ecus, 100m escudos, 100m euros, 100m guilders, 100m kwacha, 100m lire** (if Italian, **liras** if Turkish), **100m naira, 100m pesos, 100m rand** (not rands), **100m rupees** and **100m yuan** (not renminbi). To avoid confusion the *real* (plural *reais*) is set in italics.

Currencies are not set in small caps, unless they occur as words in text without figures attached: **He who pays the piper, whether in D-marks or SDRS, calls the tune.**

For a full list of currencies and currency symbols, see pages 105–110.

CURRENT and **contemporary** mean **at that time,** not necessarily **at this time.** So a series of **current prices** from 1960 to 1970 will not be in **today's prices,** just as **contemporary art** in 1800 was not **modern art. Contemporary history** is a contradiction in terms.

D

DATA are plural.

DATES. Month, day, year, in that order, with no commas:

July 5th	July 1998
Monday July 5th	1990s
July 5th 1998	July 27th–August 3rd 1998
July 5th–12th 1998	1998–99

Write
20th century, 21st century, but fifth century
20th-century ideas
a man in his 20s, and 20th anniversary
a 29-year-old, a 29-year-old man
in 100 years' time

In general give dates; **last week** or **last month** can cause confusion.
    Write **the second world war** or **the 1939–45 war**, not **world war two, II** or **2**. Similarly, prefer **the first world war** to **world war one, I** or **1**. **Post-war** and **pre-war** are hyphenated.
    See also FIGURES and HYPHENS.

DECIMATE means to destroy a proportion (originally a tenth) of a group of people or things, not to destroy them all or nearly all.

DEFINITIVE means authoritative, final, decisive; **definite** means precise, distinct.

DELIVER is transitive. So if someone is to **deliver**, he must deliver **letters, babies** or **the goods** – whether **groceries** or **what he promised.**

DEPRECATE means to **express disapproval of; depreciate** means to **belittle** or **reduce the value of. They deprecated his violent language but did not wish to depreciate the importance of his message.**

DIFFERENT from, not **to** or **than.**

DILEMMA. This is not just any old awkwardness, it is one with horns, being, properly, a form of argument (the horned syllogism) in which you find yourself committed to accept one of two propositions each of which contradicts your original contention. Hence a dilemma offers the choice between alternatives, each with equally nasty consequences.

DISCREET means **circumspect** or **prudent**; discrete means **separate** or **distinct**. Remember that "**Questions are never indiscreet. Answers sometimes are.**" (Oscar Wilde)

DISINTERESTED means **impartial**; uninterested means **bored**. ("**Disinterested curiosity is the lifeblood of civilisation.**" G.M. Trevelyan.)

DISTINCTIVE means **characteristic, serving to identify**; distinct means **definite, distinguishable, separate. Entering his room, she noticed that, as well as the distinctive smell of the cigars he always smoked, there was a faint but distinct odour of rotting fish.**

DUE TO has three meanings:
1. caused by, as in **The cancellation, due to rain, of ...** In this sense, it must follow a noun, so do not write **The match was cancelled due to rain.** If you mean **because of** and for some reason are reluctant to say it, you probably want **owing to. It was cancelled owing to rain** is all right.
2. owed to, as in **A month's salary is due to Smith.**
3. arranged or timed to, as in **The meeting is due to end at 3.30.**

E

-EABLE. See -ABLE.

EARNINGS. Do not write **earnings** when you mean **profits** (say if they are operating, gross, pre-tax or net).

-EE: employees, evacuees, detainees, referees, refugees but, please, no **attendees** (those attending), **draftees** (conscripts), **escapees** (escapers), **retirees** (the retired), or **grandees.** A **divorcee** may be male or female.

EFFECT means to **accomplish**, so **The novel effected a change in his attitude.** See also AFFECT.

EFFECTIVELY means **with effect**; if you mean **in effect**, say it. **The matter was effectively dealt with on Friday** means it was **done well** on Friday. **The matter was, in effect, dealt with on Friday** means that it was **more or less attended to** on Friday. **Effectively leaderless** would do as a description of the demonstrators in East Germany in 1989 but not those in Tiananmen Square. The devaluation of the Slovak currency in 1993, described by some as an **effective** 8%, turned out to be a rather ineffective 8%.

ENORMITY means a **crime, sin** or **monstrous wickedness.** It does not mean immensity.

ENVIRONMENT. Often unavoidable, but not a pretty word. Avoid the **business environment,** the **school environment,** the **work environment.** Try to rephrase the sentence: **business conditions, at school, at work. Surroundings** is often better.

EPICENTRE means that point on the earth's surface above the centre of an earthquake. To say that **Mr Jones was at the epicentre of the dispute** suggests that the argument took place underground.

ETHNIC GROUPS. Avoid giving offence. This should be your first concern. But also avoid mealy-mouthed euphemisms and terms that have not generally caught on despite promotion by pressure-groups. If American blacks do not wish to be called **black**, as some years ago it became plain that they no longer wished to be called **coloured**, call them **African-American**.

When writing about Spanish-speaking people in the United States, use **Hispanic** as a general term. Be specific (eg, **Mexican-American**) only if there is a possibility of confusion.

Africans may be black or white. If you mean blacks, write **blacks**. In South Africa people of mixed race are **Coloureds**.

The inhabitants of **Azerbaijan** are **Azerbaijanis**, some of whom, but not all, are **Azeris**. Those **Azeris** who live in other places, such as Iran, are not **Azerbaijanis**. Similarly, many **Croats** are not **Croatian**, and many **Serbs** not **Serbian**.

Anglo-Saxon is not a synonym for English-speaking.

The language spoken in Iran and Tajikistan is **Persian**, not **Farsi**. **Flemings** speak **Dutch**.

See also STATES, pages 140ff.

EVERY ONE refers to a number; **everyone** means **everybody**.

EX. Be careful with **ex: a Liberal ex-member** has lost his seat; **an ex-Liberal member** has lost his party.

EXCEPTIONABLE means can be taken exception to; exceptional means unusual, out of the ordinary. To claim that there has been no musical genius since Beethoven is an exceptionable remark, as there have been many other exceptional composers.

F

FACT. The fact that can usually be boiled down to **that**.

FEWER (not **less**) **than seven speeches, fewer than seven samurai.** Use **fewer**, not **less**, with numbers of individual items or people. **Less than £200, less than 700 tonnes of oil, less than a third,** because these are measured quantities or proportions, not individual items.

FIEF, not **fiefdom.**

FIGURES. Never start a sentence with a figure; write the number in words instead.

Use figures for numerals from 11 upwards, and for all numerals that include a decimal point or a fraction (eg, **4.25, 4¹/₄**). Use words for simple numerals from one to ten, except: in references to pages; in percentages (eg, **4%**); and in sets of numerals some of which are higher than ten, eg, **Deaths from this cause in the past three years were 14, 9 and 6.** It is occasionally permissible to use words rather than numbers when referring to a rough or rhetorical figure (such as **a thousand curses**).

Fractions should be hyphenated (**two-thirds, five-eighths**, etc) and, unless they are attached to whole numbers (**8¹/₂, 29⁵/₈**), spelled out in words, even when the figures are higher than ten: **He gave one-tenth of his salary to the church, one-twentieth to his mistress and one-thirtieth to his wife.** See also FRACTIONS, page 114.

Do not compare a fraction with a decimal (so avoid **The rate fell from 3¹/₂% to 3.1%**).

Fractions are more precise than decimals (3.14 neglects an infinity of figures that are embraced by ²²/₇), but your readers probably do not think so. You should therefore use fractions for rough figures (**Kenya's population is growing at 3¹/₂ a year, A hectare is 2¹/₂ acres**) and decimals for more exact ones: **The retail price index is rising at an annual rate of 10.6%.** Treat all numbers with respect but beware of phoney over-precision.

Use **m** for **million**. But spell out **billion**, which to us means **1,000m**, except in charts, where **bn** is permissible. Thus: **8m, £8m, 8 billion, DM8 billion.**

A **billion** is a thousand million, a **trillion** a thousand billion (or a million million), a **quadrillion** a thousand trillion. See also METRIC SYSTEM PREFIXES, page 124.

Use **5,000–6,000** and **5–6%; 5m–6m** (not **5–6m**), **$5m–6m;** and

5 billion–6 billion or 5bn–6bn. But **sales rose from 5m to 6m** (not 5m–6m); **estimates ranged between 5m and 6m** (not 5m–6m).

Where **to** is being used as part of a ratio, it is usually best to spell it out. Thus **They decided, by nine votes to two, to put the matter to the general assembly which voted, 27 to 19, to insist that the ratio of vodka to tomato juice in a bloody mary should be at least one to three, though the odds of this being so in most bars were put at no better than 11 to 4.** Where a ratio is being used adjectivally, figures and hyphens may be used, but only if one of the figures is greater than ten: thus a **50-20 vote, a 19-9 vote.** Otherwise, spell out the figures and use **to: a two-to-one vote, a ten-to-one likelihood.**

Do not use a hyphen or dash in place of **to** except with figures: **He received a sentence of 15–20 years in jail** but **He promised to have escaped within three to four weeks' time.**

Avoid **from 1947–50** (say **in 1947–50** or **from 1947 to 1950**) and **between 1961–65** (say **in 1961–65** or **from 1961 to 1965**).

With figures, use **a person** or **per person, a year** or **per year**, not **per caput, per capita** or **per annum.**

The style for aircraft types can be confusing. Some have hyphens in obvious places (eg, F-22, B-2 **bomber**), some in unusual places (MiG-31M) and some none at all (**Airbus** A340, BAe, RJ70). Others have both name and number (**Lockheed** P-3 **Orion**). When in doubt, use Jane's "All The World's Aircraft". Its index also includes makers' correct names.

The style for calibres is **50mm** or **105mm** with no hyphen; but **5.5-inch** and **25-pounder.**

Use the sign % instead of **per cent.** But write **percentage,** not **%age** (though in most contexts **proportion** or **share** is preferable).

See also HYPHENS, page 31ff; MEASUREMENTS, page 40; MEASURES, pages 121ff.

FINALLY. Do not use **finally** when, at the end of a series, you mean **lastly** or, in other contexts, when you mean **at last. Richard Burton**

finally marries Liz Taylor would have been all right second time round but not first.

FLAUNT means **display; flout** means **disdain**. If you **flout** this distinction you will **flaunt** your ignorance.

FOREIGN WORDS AND PHRASES. Try not to use foreign words and phrases unless there is no English alternative, which is unusual (so **a year** or **per year**, not **per annum; a person** or **per person** not **per capita; beyond one's authority** not **ultra vires;** etc). See also ITALICS and LATIN.

FORGO means **do without;** it forgoes the **e. Forego** means **go before.** A **foregone conclusion** is one that is predetermined; **a forgone conclusion** is non-existent.

FORMER: avoid wherever possible use of **the former** and **the latter.** It usually causes confusion. (See also EX.)

FORTUITOUS means **accidental,** not **fortunate** or **well-timed.**

FRACTIOUS means **peevish** or **unruly; factious** means **divisive** or produced by **faction. English soccer fans have a reputation for being both fractious and factious.**

FRANKENSTEIN was not a monster, but his creator.

FREE is an adjective or an adverb, so you cannot have or do anything **for free.** Either you have it **free** or you have it **for nothing.**

FUND is a technical term, meaning to **convert floating debt into more or less permanent debt at fixed interest.** Do not use it if you mean to **finance** or to **pay for.**

G

GENDER is a word to be applied to grammar, not people. If someone is female, that is her **sex** not her **gender**.

GENERATION: take care. You can be a second-generation Frenchman, but if you are a second-generation immigrant that means you have left the country your parents came to.

GENITIVE. Take care with the genitive. It is fine to say **a friend of Bill's**, just as you would say **a friend of mine**, so you can also say **a friend of Bill's and Hillary's**. But it is also fine to say **a friend of Bill**, or **a friend of Bill and Hillary**. What you must not say is **Bill and Hillary's friend**. If you wish to use that construction, you must say **Bill's and Hillary's friend**, which is cumbersome.

GENTLEMEN'S AGREEMENT, not **gentleman's.**

GERUND. Respect the gerund. Gerunds look like participles – **running, jumping, standing** – but are more noun-like, and should never therefore be preceded by a personal pronoun. So the following are wrong: **I was awoken by him snoring. He could not prevent them drowning. Please forgive me coming late.** Those sentences should have ended: **his snoring, their drowning, my coming late.** In other words, use the possessive adjective rather than the personal pronoun.

GET: an adaptable verb, but it has its limits. A man does not **get** sacked or promoted, he **is** sacked or promoted.

GOURMET means **epicure**; **gourmand** means **greedy-guts.**

H

HALVE is a transitive verb, so deficits can double but not **halve**. They must **be halved** or **fall by half**.

HANGING CLAUSES. If you begin a sentence with an adjectival or adverbial phrase, make sure that it qualifies the subject of the sentence. Thus, avoid: **After a fortnight's absence, your house plants will have shrivelled up.**

HEALTHY. If you think something is **desirable** or **good**, say so. Do not call it **healthy**.

HOARDS. Secreted treasures (**hoards**) are not multitudes on the move (**hordes**).

HOBSON'S CHOICE is not **the lesser of two evils**, it is **no choice at all**.

HOI POLLOI means **the many** or **the rabble** in Greek. Do not therefore write **the hoi polloi**.

HOMOGENEOUS means **of the same kind or nature**. Homogenous means **similar because of common descent**.

HOMOPHOBE. A new word, meaning someone who dislikes HOMO-SEXUALS.

HOMOSEXUAL. Since this word comes from the Greek word *homos* (same), not the Latin word *homo* (man), it applies as much to women as to men. It is therefore as daft to write **homosexuals and lesbians** as to write **people and women**.

HOPEFULLY. By all means begin an article hopefully, but never write: **Hopefully, it will be finished by Wednesday.** Try: **with luck, if all goes well, it is hoped that ...**

HYPHENS. Use hyphens as follows.

1. Fractions (whether nouns or adjectives): **two-thirds, four-fifths, one-sixth,** etc. See also FRACTIONS, page 114.

2. Most words that begin with prefixes like **ex, anti, non** and

neo: anti-aircraft, anti-fascist, anti-submarine (but anticlimax, antidote, antiseptic); **non-combatant, non-existent, non-payment, non-violent** (but **nonaligned, nonconformist, nonplussed, nonstop**); **neo-conservative, neo-liberal** (but **neoclassicism, neolithic, neologism**). But hyphens are not necessary with the prefixes **over, under** and **sub.**

Words beginning **Euro** should be hyphenated, except **Europhile, Europhobe** and **Eurosceptic.** See also EURO-TERMS.

Some words that become unmanageable with an added prefix need hyphenating: **under-secretary** and **inter-governmental.**

Antidisestablishmentarianism would, however, lose its point it if were hyphenated.

A sum followed by the word **worth** also needs a hyphen: thus, **$25m-worth of goods.**

3. Some titles:

vice-president	*but*
director-general	**deputy director**
under-secretary	**deputy secretary**
secretary-general	**district attorney**
attorney-general	**general secretary**
lieutenant-colonel	
major-general	
field-marshal	

4. To avoid ambiguities:

a little-used car	**a little used-car**
cross-complaint	**cross complaint**
high-school girl	**high schoolgirl**
fine-tooth comb (most people do not comb their teeth)	
third-world war	**third world war**

5. Adjectives formed from two or more words:
right-wing groups (*but* **the right wing** of the party)
balance-of-payments difficulties
private-sector wages
public-sector borrowing requirement
a 70-year-old judge
state-of-the-union message
value-added tax (VAT)

6. Adverbs do not need to be linked to participles or adjectives by hyphens in simple constructions: **The regiment was ill equipped**

for its task; The principle is well established; Though expensively educated, the journalist knew no grammar. But if the adverb is one of two words together being used adjectivally, a hyphen may be needed: **The ill-equipped regiment was soon repulsed; All well-established principles should be periodically challenged.** The hyphen is especially likely to be needed if the adverb is short and common, such as **ill, little, much** and **well.** Less-common adverbs, including all those that end -ly, are less likely to need hyphens: **Never employ an expensively educated journalist.** See ADVERBS.

7. Do not overdo the literary device of hyphenating words that are not usually linked: the stringing-together-of-lots-and-lots-of-words-and-ideas tendency can be tiresome.

8. Separating identical letters: **book-keeping** (but **bookseller**), **coat-tails, co-operate, unco-operative, pre-eminent, pre-empt** (but **predate, pre-condition**), **re-emerge, re-entry** (but **rearrange, reborn, repurchase**), **trans-ship.**
   Exceptions include **override, overrule, underrate, withhold.**

9. Nouns formed from prepositional verbs: **bail-out, build-up, buy-out, call-up, get-together, round-up, set-up, shake-up,** etc.

10. The quarters of the compass: **north-east(ern), south-east(ern), south-west(ern), north-west(ern), the mid-west(ern).**

11. **Makers, miners, owners** and **workers** can stand unattached and hyphen-less: **car maker, coal miner, mill owner, steel worker.** However, write **policymakers,** but **foreign-policy makers;** also **bookmaker, codemaker, peacekeeper, peacemaker.** But **trouble-maker.**

12. *One word*

airfield	businessman	forever
antibiotic	bypass	goodwill
anticlimax	cashflow	halfhearted
antidote	ceasefire	handout
antiseptic	coastguard	handpicked
antitrust	codebreaker	hardline
backlog	comeback	headache
bilingual	commonsense (adj)	hijack
blackboard	figleaf	hobnob
blueprint	foothold	kowtow

lacklustre
layoff (noun)
loophole
lopsided
lukewarm
machinegun
multilingual
nationwide
nevertheless
nonetheless
offshore
oilfield
onshore
overpaid
overrated
override
overrule
overrun

peacekeepers (-ing)
petrochemical
profitmaking
rainforest
salesforce
seabed
semiconductor
shipbuilders
shortlist
shutdown
soyabean
statewide
stockmarket
strongman
subcommittee
subcontinent
subcontract
subhuman

submachinegun
sunbelt
takeover
threshold
timetable
transatlantic
transpacific
turnout
underdog
underpaid
underrated
videocassette
videodisc
wartime
workforce
worldwide

13. Two words

ad hoc
air base
air force
aircraft carrier
any more
arm's length
ballot box

birth rate
child care
chip maker
common sense
(noun)
drug dealer (-ing)
errand boy

girl friend
health care
Land Rover
microchip maker
on to
under way
vice versa

14. Two hyphenated words

agri-business
asylum-seekers
build-up
catch-phrase
death-squads
drawing-board
end-game
end-year
faint-hearted
fund-raiser (-ing)
heir-apparent
hot-head
ice-cream
infra-red

inter-governmental
know-how
long-standing
mid-week, mid-
   August, etc
nation-state
news-stand
post-war
pre-war
pull-out (noun)
question-mark
rain-check
re-create (meaning
   create again)

re-present (meaning
   present again)
re-sort (meaning
   sort again)
starting-point
sticking-point
stumbling-block
talking-shop
task-force
think-tank
time-bomb
turning-point
working-party

15. *Three words*
ad hoc agreement
capital gains tax
chiefs of staff
half a dozen
in as much
in so far
multiple rocket launcher
nuclear power station
nuclear aircraft carrier

Three hyphenated words
brother-in-law
chock-a-block
commander-in-chief
no-man's-land
prisoners-of-war
second-in-command

16. Avoid **from 1947–50** (say **in 1947–50** or **from 1947 to 1950**) and **between 1961–65** (say in **1961–65** or **from 1961 to 1965**). Some people use dashes, not hyphens, with dates. A hyphen (or dash) should not be used instead of **to** except with figures. See also DATES, FIGURES.

HYPOTHERMIA is what kills old folk in winter. If you say it is **hyperthermia**, that means they have been carried off by heat stroke.

I

-IBLE. See -ABLE.

ILK means **same**, so **of that ilk** means **of the place of the same name as the family**, not **of that kind**. Best avoided.

IMMOLATE means to **sacrifice**, not to **burn**.

IMPORTANT. If something is important, say why and to whom. Use sparingly.

INCHOATE means **not fully developed** or **at an early stage**, and not **incoherent** or **chaotic**.

INFER. By including this word, we **imply** that it is sometimes misused. When reading this entry, you **infer** that the two highlighted words have different meanings.

INITIALS. Initials in people's names, or in companies named after them, take points (with a space between initials and name, but not between initials). Thus, **F.W. de Klerk, E.I. Du Pont de Nemours, F.W. Woolworth.** The only exceptions are for PEOPLE, COMPANIES and ORGANISATIONS that deliberately leave the points out. In general, follow the practice preferred by themselves in writing their own names. See also ABBREVIATIONS.

INTERNMENT. Generally considered a preferable penalty to **interment**: the former means **confinement**, the latter means **burial** in a grave or tomb.

INVESTIGATIONS of, not **into**.

ITALICS. Use italics for:

1. Foreign words and phrases, such as *cabinet* (French type), *chaebol, de jure, glasnost, intifada, Mitbestimmung, papabile, perestroika, ujamaa* unless they are so familiar that they have become anglicised. Thus **ad hoc, apartheid, machismo, putsch, pogrom, realpolitik, status quo,** etc, are in roman. Make sure that the meaning of any foreign word you use is clear. See also ACCENTS; ANIMALS, PLANTS, ETC; FOREIGN WORDS AND PHRASES.

2. Newspapers and periodicals. Note that only *The Economist* and *The Times* have **The** italicised. Thus the *Daily Telegraph*, the *New York Times*, the *Observer*, the *Spectator*, the *Independent*, the *Financial Times* (but *Le Monde, Die Welt, Die Zeit*). Books, pamphlets, plays, radio and television programmes are roman, with capital letters for each main word, in quotation marks. Thus: **"Pride and Prejudice"**, **"Much Ado about Nothing"**, **"Any Questions"**, **"Crossfire"**, etc. But **the Bible** and its books (**Genesis, Ecclesiastes, John,** etc) do not have inverted commas. These rules apply to footnotes as well as bodymatter.

However, book publishers generally use italics for books and pamphlets, plays, radio and television programmes.

3. Lawsuits. If abbreviated, *versus* should always be shortened to *v*, with no point after it. Thus: **Brown *v* Board of Education, Coatsworth *v* Johnson.**

4. The names of ships, aircraft, spacecraft. Thus: HMS *Illustrious, Spirit of St Louis, Challenger,* etc.

Note that a ship is **she**; a country is **it**.

J • K

JARGON. Avoid it. All sections of *The Economist* should be intelligible to all our readers, most of whom are foreigners. You may have to think harder if you are not to use jargon, but you can still be precise. Technical terms should be used in their proper context; do not use them out of it. In many instances simple words can do the job of **exponential** (try **fast**), **interface** (**frontier** or **border**), and so on. Avoid, above all, the kind of jargon that tries either to dignify nonsense with seriousness (**Working in an empowering environment**, a topic discussed at an Economist conference) or to obscure the truth (**We shall not launch the ground offensive until we have attrited the Republican Guard to the point when they no longer have an effective offensive capacity** – the Pentagon's way of saying that the allies would not fight on the ground until they had killed so many Iraqis that the others would not attack). What was meant by the Israeli defence ministry when it issued the following press release remains unclear: **The United States and Israel now possess the capability to conduct real-time simulations with man in the loop for full-scale theatre missile defence architectures for the Middle East.**

JUST. If you can write **only** instead, do so.

●

KEY. Keys may be **major** or **minor**, but not **low**. Few of the decisions, people, industries described as **key** are truly **indispensable**, and fewer still **open locks**.

KNOWLEDGEABLE: verbs are -ableable, but not nouns (with some exceptions such as **profitable**). Try **well informed**.

L

LAG. If you **lag** transitively, you lag a pipe or a loft. Front-runners, rates of growth, fourth-quarter profits and so on **lag behind**.

LAST. The last issue of *The Economist* implies our extinction; prefer **last week's** or the **latest** issue. Likewise avoid the **last** issue of *Foreign Affairs*: prefer the **latest, current, most recent** or (eg) **June** issue, or **this month's** or **last month's** issue.

Last year, in 2000, means 1999; if you mean the 12 months up to the time of writing, write **the past year.** The same goes for the **past** month, **past** week, **past** (not **last**) ten years. See also DATES.

LIFESTYLE: prefer **way of life**.

LIGHT-YEAR. A light-year is a measurement of distance, not of time. It is the approximate distance travelled by light in one year.

Thus: 1 light-year = 5.88×10^{12} miles
9.46×10^{12} km

LIKE governs nouns and pronouns, not verbs and clauses. So **as in America** not **like in America**. But **authorities like Fowler and Gowers** is an acceptable alternative to **authorities such as Fowler and Gowers**.

LOCATE, in all its forms, can usually be replaced by something less ugly. **The missing scientist was located** means he was **found**. **The diplomats will meet at a secret location** means either that they will meet **in a secret place** or that they will meet **secretly**. **A company located in Texas** is simply **a company in Texas**.

LOWER CASE. See CAPITALS.

M

MASTERFUL means **imperious**. **Masterly** means **skilled**.

MAXIMISE means to make as great as possible. Weight-lifting can maximise your biceps, but not your health.

MAY and **might** are not always interchangeable, and you may want **may** more often than you think. If in doubt, try **may** first.

You need **might** in the past tense. **I may go to Leeds later** becomes, in the past, **I might have gone to Leeds later**. And in indirect past speech it becomes **I said I might go to Leeds later**.

Conditional sentences using the subjunctive also need **might**. Thus **If I were to go to Leeds, I might have to stand all the way**. This could be rephrased **If I go to Leeds, I may have to stand all the way**. Conditional sentences stating something contrary to fact, however, need **might**: **If pigs had wings, birds might raise their eyebrows**.

Do not write **Bill Clinton might be president of the United States, but he does not eat broccoli**. It should be **Bill Clinton may be president of the United States, but he does not eat broccoli**. Only if you are putting forward a hypothesis that may or may not be true are **may** and **might** interchangeable. Thus **If Al Gore always eats his broccoli, he may** (or **might**) **become president of the United States**.

MEASUREMENTS. In most contexts that are not American or British, prefer **hectares** to **acres**, **kilometres** (or **km**) to **miles**, **metres** to **yards**, **litres** to **gallons**, **kilos** to **lb**, **tonnes** to **tons**, **Celsius** to **Fahrenheit**, etc. Regardless of which you choose, you should give an equivalent, on first use, in the other units: **It was hoped that after improvements to the engine the car would give 20km to the litre (47 miles per American gallon) compared with its present average of 15km per litre**.

Remember that in few countries do you now buy petrol in imperial gallons. In America it is sold in American gallons; in most places it is sold in litres.

See also MEASURES, pages 121ff.

MEDIA: prefer **press and television** or, if the context allows it, just **press**. If you have to use the **media**, remember the word is plural.

METAPHORS. "A newly invented metaphor assists thought by evoking a visual image," said George Orwell, "while on the other hand a metaphor which is technically 'dead' (eg, iron resolution) has in effect reverted to being an ordinary word and can generally be used without loss of vividness. But in between these two classes there is a huge dump of wornout metaphors which are merely used because they save people the trouble of inventing phrases for themselves."

Every issue of *The Economist* contains scores of metaphors:

a trail of crushed rivals
billing and cooing politicians
a smaller helping of Europe's manifest destiny
a project falling at the first hurdle
a weaker grip on monetary policy
a track record on inflation
tabloid reporters lapping up stories
a report leaving the door ajar
irresistible forces about to meet an immovable object
a roadblock in the path of reform
investors crying foul
a presidential u-turn
water off a duck's back in the Senate
a door slammed shut in China
a blind eye turned in Taiwan

an investor jumping the gun
heat off in America
the reins of power in Japan
a bargaining chip in South Africa
a honeymoon (soon to be over)
an iron-clad argument
foot-dragging
a run-up to the election
a counterweight to German domination
a shadow cast over the future
bureaucratic barriers
uprooted democracy
grass-roots organisations
mainstream conservatives
young turks
a crash-course in capitalism
grinding poverty
flabby banks getting into shape
politicians turning a deaf ear
a binge of brand acquisitions

Some of these are tired, and will therefore tire the reader. Most are so exhausted that they may be considered dead, and are therefore permissible. But use all metaphors, dead or alive, sparingly, otherwise you will make trouble for yourself.

An issue of *The Economist* chosen at random had a **package cutting the budget deficit, the administration loth to sign on to higher targets, liberals accused of playing politics on the court (Supreme, not tennis),** only to find in the next sentence that **the boot was on the other foot, the lure of eastern Germany as a springboard to the struggling markets of Eastern Europe, West Europeanness helping to dilute an image,** someone **finding a pretext to stall the process** before looking for **a few integrationist crumbs, an end-of-millennium spring clean** that became in the next sentence **a stalking-horse for greater spending,** and **Michelin axing jobs in painful surgery** in order stay at **the top of a league table.** Soon the Michelin man **was plunging his company even further in to debt,** though if it were **to stay afloat his ambitions would have to be deflated.** Little wonder other French firms **were striking out abroad.** The reader had to **go down to the seas again** two pages on when a **flotilla of mutual and quoted life-assurance outfits were confident of surviving turbulent waters. The galleons were afloat,** but **the medium-sized and smaller mutuals** quickly turned into **fodder for domestic and foreign predators.** Further on, **banks going to the altar in the expectation of a tax-free dowry** saw it become a **sweetener** in the next sentence and the bill that delivered it transformed into a **panacea.** Those who wanted to learn about Japanese equity financing were told of a **stockmarket crawling back** (not on its feet, it was explained) **towards its old high,** of **commercial banks keeping the wolf from the door** and, three paragraphs later, of **the stockmarket's double whammy. One whammy was a crash which made a big dent in shares, the other blew a hole (a gaping one) in the so-called *tokkin* fund**s. On, on went the reader past **masked bunglings, key measures, money-supply growth out of hand, a haunted Bank of Japan redoubling its**

squeeze, banks slashing growth lest they found themselves on a tight leash before being cracked down on. Few could have been surprised to learn at the end of the article that **another dose of higher interest rates might be forced on the banks if the present inflationary symptoms turned into measles-like spots, and if the apothecaries at the finance ministry agreed with the diagnosis.**

These two sentences, used as an opening paragraph to arrest the attention of the readers of A.N. *Other* newspaper, found their way past its subeditors and into print:

Bulgaria is on its knees. A long-simmering economic crisis has erupted, gripping the country in a fierce and unrelenting embrace.

Another publication lamented:

Mr Clinton has had to pull the plug on a plan that had been tarred as a bail-out for an incompetent regime and the Wall Street fat cats who invested in it.

METE. You may **mete out** punishment, but if it is to fit the crime it is **meet.**

MILLIONAIRE. The time has gone when girls in the Bois du Boulogne would think that the term **millionaire** adequately described the man who broke the Bank at Monte Carlo. If you wish to use it, make it plain that **millionaire** refers to income (in dollars or pounds), not to capital. Otherwise try **plutocrat** or **rich man.**

MINIMISE means to make as small as possible; you cannot **slightly minimise** something.

MITIGATES mollifies, **militates** does the opposite.

MONOPOLY. A **monopolist** is the sole seller; a monopoly buyer is a **monopsonist.**

MOVE: do not use if you mean **decision, bid, deal** or something more precise. But **move** rather than **relocate.**

N

Names

ARAB. Try to leave out the **al-**. If the name looks odd without it, include it (lower case, followed by hyphen).

BANGLADESHI, PAKISTANI. If the name includes the Islamic definite article, (**ur** in Bangladeshi, **ul** in Pakistani), it should be lower case and without any hyphens: **Mujib ur Rahman, Zia ul Haq.** (**Sadruddin, Mohieddin** and **Saladin** are single words.)

CHINESE. In general follow the Pinyin spelling, which has replaced the old Wade-Giles system, except for people from the past, and people and places outside mainland China. **Peking** is therefore **Beijing** and **Mao** is **Zedong**, not **Tse-tung**.
There are no hyphens in Pinyin spelling. So:

Deng Xiaoping	*But*
Guangdong (Kwangtung)	Chiang Kai-shek
Guangzhou (Canton)	Hong Kong
Hu Yaobang	Li Ka-shing
Jiang Zemin	Lee Teng-hui
Jiang Qing (Mrs Mao)	
Mao Zedong (Tse-tung)	
Qingdao (Tsingtao)	
Tianjin (Tientsin)	
Xinjiang (Sinkiang)	
Zhao Ziyang	

The family name in China comes first, so **Jiang Zemin** becomes **Mr Jiang** on a later mention.
Names from **Singapore, Korea, Vietnam** have no hyphens: **Lee Kuan Yew, Kim Jong Il, Ho Chi Minh**. Again, the family name comes first.
See also FOREIGN WORDS AND PHRASES; PEOPLE; TITLES.

DUTCH. If using first name and surname together, **vans** and **dens** are lower case: **Dries van Agt** and **Joop den Uyl**. But without their first names they become **Mr Van Agt** and **Mr Den Uyl**; **Hans van der Broek** becomes **Mr Van der Broek**. These rules do not always apply to Dutch names in Belgium and South Africa; **Karel Van Miert**, for instance (as well as **Mr Van Miert**).

FRENCH. Any **de** is likely to be lower case, unless it starts a sentence. **De Gaulle** goes up; **Charles de Gaulle** goes down. So does **Yves-Thibault de Silguy.**

GERMAN. Any **von** is likely to be upper case only at the start of a sentence.

ITALIAN. Any **De** is likely to be upper case, but there are exceptions, so check.

RUSSIAN. Each of the different approaches to transliterating Russian has its drawbacks. The following rules of thumb are chosen chiefly for reasons of simplicity, not phonetic accuracy.

1. No y before e: **Belarus,** *perestroika.* Exception: if the e starts the word: **Yeltsin, Yevgeny.**

2. Where pronunciation demands it, use y before a at the start of a word, but not at the end: **Yavlinsky, Yakovlev, Alia** (not **Aliya**). But **Chechnya.**
Special case: the president of Turkmenistan is **Saparmurat Niyazov.**

3. Anything pronounced yo is usually spelled e: **Fedorov, Gorbachev.**

4. With words ending -ski, -skii or -sky, choose -sky. But with all other words ending -i, -ii or -y, choose -i. Thus **Zhirinovsky** and **Tchaikovsky,** but **Bolshoi, Rutskoi, Yuri.** Exceptions: **Grigory** (because of the association with Gregory) and **Nizhny Novgorod.**

5. Replace dzh with j. So: **Jokar** (**Dudaev**), **Jaba** (**Iosseliani**).

UKRAINIAN. Ukrainians are engaging in retransliterating Russian versions of their words, often several times. It is impossible to keep up, so go for the familiar, if there is one. Ukrainian has no g, so it is **Yvhen** (not **Yevgeny**), **Ihor** (not **Igor**) and **Luhansk** (not **Lugansk**).

NONE usually takes a singular verb. So does **neither** (or **either**) **A nor** (or **or**) **B,** unless B is plural, as in **Neither the Dutchman nor the Danes have done it,** where the verb agrees with the element closest to it.

NOR means **and not,** so should not be preceded by **and.**

NOT ONLY. This should appear next to the item it qualifies. **His sister loved not only him** and **his sister not only loved him** have different meanings. When used with **but also**, it must either follow the verb or the verb must be repeated, eg, **he not only hurt her feelings but also hurt her pride**, better phrased as **he hurt not only her feelings but also her pride** (see the advice given under BOTH ... AND).

NUMBERS. See FIGURES, pages 27–28; MEASUREMENTS, page 40; MEASURES pages 121ff.

O

ONE. Try to avoid **one** as a personal pronoun. **You** will often do instead.

ONLY. Put **only** as close as you can to the words it qualifies. Thus, **These animals mate only in June.** To say **They only mate in June** implies that in June they do nothing else. Always prefer **only** to **just.**

ON TO not **onto.**

OVERWHELM means **submerge utterly, crush, bring to sudden ruin.** Majority votes, for example, seldom do any of these things.

OXYMORON. An **oxymoron** is not an unintentional contradiction in terms but **a figure of speech in which contradictory terms are deliberately combined,** as in bitter-sweet, cruel kindness, sweet sorrow.

P

PEOPLE. Call them what they want to be called, short of festooning them with titles. Use full stops (points) after initials.
Here are some names which may present problems.

Heidar Aliev
Kofi Annan
Yasser Arafat
Hafez Assad
Omar el Bashir
Zine El Abidine Ben Ali
Chadli Benjedid
Ritt Bjerregaard
Boutros Boutros-Ghali
Zbigniew Brzezinski
Leopoldo Calvo-Sotelo
Viktor Chernomyrdin
Poul Dalsager
Carlo De Benedetti
Gaston Defferre
Gianni De Michelis
Ciriaco De Mita
Yves-Thibault de Silguy
Carlo Ripa di Meana
Lawrence Eagleburger
Garret FitzGerald
Yegor Gaidar
Gandhi
Hans-Dietrich Genscher
Felipe Gonzalez
Mikhail Gorbachev
Jorg Haider
Elias Hrawi
Saddam Hussein
Radovan Karadzic
Ahmad Khomeini
Jeane Kirkpatrick
Vaclav Klaus
Reinhard Klimmt
Alexander Lukashenka

Thabo Mbeki
Slobodan Milosevic
François Mitterrand
Ratko Mladic
Mahathir Mohamad
Daniel arap Moi
Hosni Mubarak
Muhammad (unless it is part
   of the name of someone who
   spells it differently)
Nursultan Nazarbaev
Jawaharlal Nehru
Benjamin Netanyahu
Saparmurat Niyazov
Gaafar Numeiri
Mammar Qaddafi
Ali Akbar Rafsanjani
Edzard Reuter
Nikolai Ryzhkov
Andrei Sakharov
Ali Abdullah Saleh
Wolfgang Schäuble
Yitzhak Shamir
Edward Shevardnadze
Banharn Silpa-archa
George Shultz
Mario Soares
Adolfo Suarez
Alexander Solzhenitsyn
Atal Behari Vajpayee
Hans-Jochen Vogel
Abdurrahman Wahid
Caspar Weinberger
Vladimir Zhirinovsky
Gennady Zyuganov

See also FOREIGN WORDS AND PHRASES; NAMES; SPELLING; TITLES.

PER CENT is not the same as a percentage point. A fall from 4% to 2% is a drop of 2 percentage points, or of 50%, but not of 2%. Nothing can fall, or be devalued, by more than 100%. If something trebles, it increases by 200%.

PERCOLATE means to pass **through**, not **up** or **down**.

PERSPICACITY and **perspicuity** should be the twin aims of writers: an acuteness of understanding coupled with lucidity of expression.

PHASE. When discussing incomes policies, monetary unions, extended plans, etc, prefer **stage** to **phase**.

PHONE: permissible, if used sparingly, but prefer **telephone**.

PLACES. Use English forms when they are in common use: **Basle, Cologne, Leghorn, Lower Saxony, Lyons, Marseilles, Naples, Nuremberg, Turin.** And English rather than American – **Rockefeller Centre, Pearl Harbour** – unless the place name is part of a company name, such as **Rockefeller Center Properties Inc.** But follow local practice when a country expressly changes its name, or the names of rivers, towns, etc, within it. Thus **Almaty** not **Alma Ata; Chemnitz** not **Karl-Marx-Stadt; Chennai** not **Madras; Côte d'Ivoire** not **Ivory Coast; Mumbai** not **Bombay; Myanmar** not **Burma; Nizhny Novgorod** not **Gorky; St Petersburg** not **Leningrad;** and **Yangon** not **Rangoon.**

Zaire has now reverted to **Congo.** In contexts where there can be no confusion with the former French country of the same name, plain **Congo** will do. But if there is any risk of misunderstanding, call it **Congo-Kinshasa.** The other Congo should always be **Congo-Brazzaville.** The river is now also the **Congo.** The people of either country are also **Congolese.**

Do not use the definite article before **Krajina, Lebanon, Piedmont, Punjab, Sudan, Transkei** and **Ukraine,** but it is **the Caucasus, The Gambia, The Hague, the Maghreb, the Netherlands** – and **La Paz, Le Havre, Los Angeles,** etc. See also COUNTRIES AND THEIR INHABITANTS, pages 20–21, and STATES, ETC, pages 140ff.

Do not use the names of capital cities as synonyms for their governments. **Britain will send a gunboat** is fine, but **London will send a gunboat** suggests that this will be the action of the people of London alone. To write **Washington and Moscow now differ only in**

their approach to Havana is absurd.

Although the place is **Western** (or **Eastern**) **Europe,** the people are **West** or **East Europeans.**

Here are the spellings of some common problematic place names.

Abkhazia
Argentina (adj and
  people Argentine,
  not Argentinian)
Ashgabat
Azerbaijan
Baden-Württemberg
Baghdad
Bahrain
Bangladesh
Basle
Belarus
Beqaa
Bophuthatswana
Bosnia & Hercegovina
Bosporus
Brittany
Cameroon
Cape Town
Caribbean
Cincinnati
Colombia (South
  America)
Columbia (univer-
  sity, District of);
  British Columbia
Cracow
Dar es Salaam
Dhaka
Djibouti
Dominica
  (Caribbean island)
Dominican
  Republic
  (part of another
  island)

El Salvador,
  Salvadorean
Gettysburg
Gothenburg
Grozny
Gujarat, Gujarati
Guyana (but French
  Guiana)
Hanover
Harare
Hercegovina
Hong Kong (but
  one word in
  Hongkong and
  Shanghai Banking
  Corporation)
Issyk-Kul
Jeddah
KaNgwane
Katmandu
Kazakhstan
Kirgizstan
Krajina
Kuwait city
KwaNdebele
KwaZulu-Natal
Luhansk
Luxembourg
Macau
Mafikeng
Mauritania
Middlesbrough
Mpumalanga
  (formerly Eastern
  Transvaal)
Nagorno-Karabakh

Nizhny Novgorod
North Rhine-
  Westphalia
Nuremberg
Philippines (the
  people are
  Filipinos
  and Filipinas)
Phnom Penh
Pittsburgh
Pyrenees, Pyrenean
Quezon City
Reykjavik
Romania
Salzburg
St Petersburg
Sebastopol
Sindh
Srebrenica
Sri Lanka
Strasbourg
Suriname
Taipei
Tajikistan
Teesside
Tehran
Tigray, Tigrayan
Transdniestria
Uzbekistan
Valletta
Zepa
Zepce

PLANE. This is a **tool,** a **surface** or, if it flies, an **aeroplane, aircraft** or **airliner** (not an **airplane**). **Warplane,** however, is allowed.

PLANTS. See ANIMALS, PLANTS, ETC.

PLURALS. No rules here. The spelling of the following plurals may be decided by either practice or derivation.

-oes

archipelagoes	heroes	salvoes
buffaloes	innuendoes	tomatoes
cargoes	mementoes	tornadoes
desperadoes	mosquitoes	torpedoes
echoes	mottoes	vetoes
embargoes	noes	volcanoes
haloes	potatoes	

-os

commandos	librettos	radios
dynamos	manifestos	silos
embryos	mulattos	solos
Eskimos	oratorios	sopranos
fiascos	peccadillos	stilettos
folios	pianos	studios
ghettos	provisos	virtuosos
impresarios	quangos	

-ums

conundrums	moratoriums	stadiums
crematoriums	nostrums	symposiums
curriculums	quorums	ultimatums
forums	referendums	vacuums

-a

addenda	data	memoranda
bacteria	errata	phenomena
consortia	genera (plural of	quanta
corpora (plural of	genus)	sanatoria
corpus)	media (but mediums	spectra
corrigenda	communicate with	strata
criteria	the spirit world)	

-uses

buses	fetuses	geniuses
caucuses	focuses	prospectuses
circuses		

-i

alumni	fungi	stimuli
bacilli	graffiti	termini
cacti	nuclei	

-s

agendas	milieus	quotas
arenas	panaceas	

-ae

amoebae	lacunae	vertebrae
formulae	nebulae	

-ves / -fs

-ves	-fs
calves	dwarfs
hooves	handkerchiefs
scarves	roofs
wharves	turfs

-eaus / -eaux

-eaus	-eaux
bureaus (*but* bureaux de change)	chateaux
plateaus	
tableaus	

-es

amanuenses	bases	oases
analyses	crises	synopses
antitheses	hypotheses	

Note. Indexes (of books); indices are indicators of index numbers. Appendixes (anatomical variety); use appendices for the literary sort.

PRECIPITOUS means **extremely steep**; a rash or hasty action is **precipitate. Precipitate share dealings led to a precipitous drop in prices.**

PREMIER, as a noun, should be confined to the first ministers of the Canadian provinces, German *Länder* and other sub-national states. Do not use it as a synonym for the prime minister of a country.

PREPOSITIONS at the end of sentences are permissible: **an example such as this is a good one to go by,** rather than **an example such as this is a good one by which to go.** But avoid **up to,** which can mean anything.

PRESENTLY means **soon**, not **at present**. "Presently Kep opened the door of the shed, and let out Jemima Puddle-Duck." (Beatrix Potter)

PREVARICATE means **evade the truth**; procrastinate means **delay**.

PRISTINE means **in its original** or **former condition**, not **pure** or **clean**.

PROBLEM. The problem with problem is it is overused, so much so that it is becoming a problem word.

PROCESS. A word properly applied to the Arab-Israeli peace affair, because it was meant to be evolutionary, but now often used in place of **talks**.

Proof-reading

Look for errors in the following categories.

1. "Typos", which include misspelt words, punctuation mistakes, wrong numbers, transposed words or sentences.
2. Bad word breaks (see page 58).
3. Layout mistakes: wrongly positioned text (including captions, headings, folios, running heads) or illustrations, incorrect line spacing, missing items, widows (short lines at the top of a page).
4. Wrong fonts: errors in the use of italic, bold, etc.

Additionally, if the text contains cross-references to numbered pages or illustrations, the proof-reader is usually responsible for inserting the correct reference at page proof stage, and for checking cross-references.

The most effective way of proof-reading is to read the text several times, each time with a different focus, rather than attempting to carry out all checks in one go. This helps concentration and makes it easier to detect inconsistencies which are usually the sign of an error.

PROOF-READING MARKS. Proof-reading marks are illustrated on the following pages. The intention of these marks is to identify, precisely and concisely, the nature of an error and the correction required. When corrections are extensive or complex, it is usually better to spell out, in full, the correct form of the text rather than leave the typesetter to puzzle over a string of hieroglyphs, however immaculately drawn and ordered. Be careful to mark all proof corrections clearly, keeping all letters separate, and write them in the margin.

INSTRUCTION	TEXTUAL MARK	MARGINAL MARK AND NOTES
Correction is concluded	None	╱ Make after each correction
Leave unchanged	under characters to remain	⊘
Remove extraneous marks	Encircle marks to be removed	✕ eg, film or paper edges visible between lines on bromide proofs
Push down risen spacing material	Encircle blemish	⊥
Refer to appropriate authority anything of doubtful accuracy	Encircle word(s) affected	⊙?
Insert in text the matter indicated in the margin	⋏ (caret mark)	New matter followed by ⋏
Delete	╱ through character(s) or ⊢——⊣ through words to be deleted	⌒⌐
Delete and close up	⌒╱ through character(s) or ⊢≈⊣ through characters, eg, or̶, characte̶r̶ter	⌒⌐
Close up – delete space	⌒‿	⌒‿

INSTRUCTION	TEXTUAL MARK	MARGINAL MARK AND NOTES
Substitute character or substitute part of one or more words	through character / or ⌐————/ through words	new character or new word(s)
Wrong font. Replace by characters of correct font	Encircle character(s) to be changed	⊗ or w.f.
Correct damaged character(s)	Encircle character(s) to be changed	✕
Set in or change to roman type	Encircle character(s) to be changed	Rom.
Set in or change to italic	——————— under character(s) to be set or changed	⌐⌐⌐/
Set in or change to capital letters	════════ under character(s) to be set or changed	≡
Set in or change to small capital letters	═══════ under character(s) to be set or changed	═
Set in or change to capital letters for initial letters and small capital letters for the rest of the words	≡ under initial letters ═ under rest of word(s)	════════ ═
Set in or change to bold type	∿∿∿∿∿ under character(s) to be set or changed	∿∿∿ or bold
Set in or change to bold italic type	∿∿∿∿∿ under character(s) to be set or changed	⌐⌐/∿
Change capital letters to lower case letters	Encircle character(s) to be changed	≢ or l.c.
Change italic to upright type	Encircle character(s) to be changed	⌐⌐/

INSTRUCTION	TEXTUAL MARK	MARGINAL MARK AND NOTES
Invert type	Encircle character to be changed	↶
Substitute or insert character in "superior" position	/ through character _or_ ⋏ where required	⅄ under character eg ⅄
Substitute separate letters for ligature	⊢————⊣	Write out separate letters
Substitute or insert full stop or decimal point	/ through character _or_ ⋏ where required	⊙
Substitute or insert colon	/ through character _or_ ⋏ where required	⊙
Substitute or insert semi-colon	/ through character _or_ ⋏ where required	;
Insert space	⌖	⌖
Equal space	| between words or letters	⤬
Reduce space	⌐ between words or letters	⌐
Close up to normal interline spacing	(each side of column linking lines)	The textual marks extend into the margin
Take over character(s), word(s) or line to next line, column or page	⎡——	The textual mark surrounds the matter to be taken over and extends into the margin
Take back character(s), word(s) or line to next line, column or page	——⎤	The textual mark surrounds the matter to be taken over and extends into the margin

INSTRUCTION	TEXTUAL MARK	MARGINAL MARK AND NOTES
Substitute or insert oblique	/ through character or / where required	
Start new paragraph		
Run on (no new paragraph)		
Transpose characters or words	between characters or words, numbered when necessary	
Transpose a number or characters or words	3 2 1	1 2 3 The vertical strokes are made through the characters or words to be transposed and numbered in sequence
Transpose lines		
Transpose a number of lines	———— 3 ———— 2 ———— 1	Rules extend from the margin into the text with each line to be transplanted numbered in the correct sequence
Centre	enclosing matter to be centred	[ ]
Indent		Give the amount of the indent in the original mark
Move to the left	|←[xxxx]	Give the amount of the indent in the original mark
Abbreviation or figure to be spelt out in full	Encircle matter to be altered	spell out
Insert single or double quotes	/ where required	ʼ ʼ ʼʼ ʼʼ

Proof-reading (continued)

WORD BREAKS. It may be necessary to break words, using a hyphen, at the end of lines. Computer word-processing programs come with standard hyphenation rules but these can always be changed or over-ruled. Ideally, the aim should be to make these breaks as undisrup-tive as possible, so that the reader does not stumble or falter. Whenever possible, the word should be broken so that, helped by the context, the reader can anticipate the whole word from the part of it given before the break. Here are some useful principles for deciding how to break a word.

1. Words that are already hyphenated should be broken at the hyphen, not given a second hyphen.
2. Words can be broken according to either their derivation (the British convention) or their pronunciation (the US convention): thus, **aristo-cracy** (UK) or **aristoc-racy** (US), **melli-fluous** (UK) or **mellif-luous** (US). See PART II for American usage.
3. Words of one syllable should not be broken.
4. Words of five or fewer characters should not be broken.
5. At least three characters must be taken over to the next line.
6. Words should not be broken so that their identity is confused or their identifying sound is distorted: thus, avoid **wo-men**, or **fo-ist**.
7. Personal names should not be broken.
8. Figures should not be broken or separated from their unit of mea-surement.
9. A word formed with a prefix or suffix should be broken at that point: thus, **bi-furcated, ante-diluvian, convert-ible**.
10. If a breakable word contains a double consonant, split it at that point: thus, **as-sess, ship-ping, prob-lem**.

PROPAGANDA (which is singular) means **a systematic effort to spread doctrine or opinions**. It is not a synonym for **lies**.

PROPER NOUNS: if they have adjectives, use them. Thus a **Californian** (not **California**) **judge**, the **Pakistani** (not **Pakistan**) **government**, the **Texan** (not **Texas**) **press**.

PROTEST. Objectors protest that a decision is unfair, or they protest at or against it. **Employers have protested against the examination boards' decision to take no account of spelling in A-level marking systems** is right; **The NUT protested the penalisation of children from ethnic minorities for writing poor English** is wrong.

Punctuation

APOSTROPHES. Use the normal possessive ending **'s** after singular words or names that end in **s**: **boss's, caucus's, Delors's, St James's, Jones's, Shanks's.** Use it after plurals that do not end in **s**: **children's, Frenchmen's, media's.**

Use the ending **s'** on plurals that end in **s** – **Danes', bosses', Joneses'** – including plural names that take a singular verb, eg, **Reuters', Barclays', Stewarts & Lloyds', Salomon Brothers'.**

Although singular in other respects, the United States, the United Nations, the Philippines, etc, have a plural possessive apostrophe: eg, **What will the United States' next move be?**

Peoples' = of peoples. **People's** = of (the) people.

Try to avoid using **Lloyd's** (the insurance market) as a possessive; it poses an insoluble problem. The vulnerable part of the hero of the Trojan war is best described as an **Achilles** heel.

Do not put apostrophes into decades: the **1990s** not the **1990's.**

BRACKETS. If a whole sentence is within brackets, put the full stop inside.

Square brackets should be used for interpolations in direct quotations: **"Let them [the poor] eat cake."** To use ordinary curved brackets implies that the words inside them were part of the original.

COLONS. Use a colon "to deliver the goods that have been invoiced in the preceding words" (Fowler). **They brought presents: gold, frankincense and oil at $35 a barrel.**

Use a colon before a whole quoted sentence, but not before a quotation that begins mid-sentence. **She said: "It will never work."** He retorted that it had "always worked before".

Use a colon for antithesis or "gnomic contrasts" (Fowler). **Man proposes: God disposes.**

COMMAS. Use commas as an aid to understanding. Too many in one sentence can be confusing.

It is not necessary to put a comma after a short phrase at the start of a sentence if no natural pause exists there: **On August 2nd he invaded. Next time the world will be prepared.** But a breath, and so a comma, is needed after longer passages: **When it was plain that he had his eyes on Saudi Arabia as well as Kuwait, America responded.**

Use two commas, or none at all, when inserting a clause in the middle of a sentence. Thus, do not write: **Use two commas, or none at all when inserting ...** or **Use two commas or none at all, when inserting ...**

If the clause ends with a bracket, which is not uncommon (this one does), the bracket should be followed by a comma.

Do not put a comma before **and** at the end of a sequence of items unless one of the items includes another **and**. Thus **The doctor suggested an aspirin, half a grapefruit and a cup of broth.** But **He ordered scrambled eggs, whisky and soda, and a selection from the trolley.** But American usage is different; see PART II.

Commas can alter the sense of a sentence. To write **Mozart's 40th symphony, in G minor**, with commas indicates that this symphony was written in G minor. Without commas, **Mozart's 40th symphony in G minor** suggests he wrote 39 other symphonies in G minor.

Do not put commas after question marks, even when they would be separated by quotation marks: **"May I have a second helping?" he asked.**

Commas in dates: none.

DASHES. You can use dashes in pairs for parenthesis, but not more than one pair per sentence, ideally not more than one pair per paragraph. (See also HYPHENS.)

Use a dash to introduce an explanation, amplification, paraphrase, particularisation or correction of what immediately precedes it.

Use it to gather up the subject of a long sentence.

Use it to introduce a paradoxical or whimsical ending to sentences.

Do not use the dash as a punctuation maid-of-all-work (Gowers).

FULL STOPS. Use plenty. They keep sentences short. This helps the reader.

Do not use full stops in ABBREVIATIONS or at the end of headings.

INVERTED COMMAS (QUOTATION MARKS). Use single ones only for quotations within quotations. Thus: **"When I say 'immediately', I mean some time before April," said the spokesman.**

When a quotation is indented and set in smaller type than the main bodymatter, do not put inverted commas around it.

For the relative placing of quotation marks and punctuation, follow Hart's rules. If an extract ends with a full stop or question-mark, put the punctuation before the closing inverted commas. **His maxim was that "love follows laughter." In this spirit came his opening gambit: "What's the difference between a buffalo and a bison?"** If a complete sentence in quotes comes at the end of a longer sentence, the final stop should be inside the inverted commas. Thus, **The answer was, "You can't wash your hands in a buffalo." She replied, "Your jokes are execrable."**

If the quotation does not include any punctuation, the closing inverted commas should precede any punctuation marks that the sentence requires. Thus: **She had already noticed that the "young man" looked about as young as the New Testament is new.** Although he had been described as "fawnlike in his energy and playfulness", "a stripling with all the vigour and freshness of youth", and even as "every woman's dream toyboy", he struck his companion-to-be as the kind of old man warned of by her mother as "not safe in taxis". **Where, now that she needed him, was "Mr Right"?**

When a quotation is broken off and resumed after such words as **he said**, ask yourself whether it would naturally have had any punctuation at the point where it is broken off. If the answer is yes, a comma is placed within the quotation marks to represent this. Thus, **"If you'll let me see you home," he said, "I think I know where we can find a cab."** The comma after **home** belongs to the quotation and so comes within the inverted commas, as does the final full stop.

But if the words to be quoted are continuous, without punctuation at the point where they are broken, the comma should be outside the inverted commas. Thus, **"My bicycle", she assured him, "awaits me."**

See pages 87–89 for American usage.

QUESTION-MARKS. Except in sentences that include a question in inverted commas, question-marks always come at the end of the sentence. Thus: **Where could he get a drink, he wondered?**

SEMI-COLONS. Semi-colons should be used to mark a pause longer than a comma and shorter than a full stop. Don't overdo them.

Use them to distinguish phrases listed after a colon if commas will not do the job clearly. Thus, **They agreed on only three points: the ceasefire should be immediate; it should be internationally supervised, preferably by the OAU; and a peace conference should be held, either in Geneva or in Ouagadougou.**

R

RACISM. As a general rule, a person's race, colour or creed should be mentioned only when relevant. See also ETHNIC GROUPS.

REAL. Is it really necessary? When used to mean **after taking inflation into account**, it is legitimate. In other contexts (**Investors are showing real interest in the country, but Bolivians wonder if real prosperity will ever arrive**), it is often better left out.

REBUT and **refute** mean **to put to flight**, or **disprove**, in argument. They are not synonyms for **deny**. ("**Shakespeare never has six lines together without a fault. Perhaps you may find seven: but this does not refute my general assertion.**" Samuel Johnson)

REGRETTABLY means it is to be regretted that; someone who shows regret is behaving **regretfully**. It is regrettably true that few people respond regretfully when told they have dropped some litter.

RELATIONSHIP is a long word often better replaced by **relations**. **The two countries hope for a better relationship** means **The two countries hope for better relations**.

RELATIVE: fine as an adjective, but as a noun prefer **relation**.

REPORT on, not **into.**

S

SAME: often superfluous. If your sentence contains **on the same day that**, try **on the day that**.

SCOTCH. To **scotch** means to **disable**, not to **destroy**. ("**We have scotched the snake, not killed it**"). The people may be Scotch, Scots or Scottish (whisky is **Scotch**); choose as you like. **Scot-free** means **free from payment of a fine** (or **punishment**), not **free from Scotsmen**.

SECTOR: try **industry** instead or, for example, **banks** instead of **banking sector**.

SEQUESTERED means **secluded**. **Sequestrated** means **confiscated** or **made bankrupt**.

SEXISM. It is often possible to phrase sentences so that they neither give offence to women nor become hideously complicated. Using the plural can be helpful. Thus **Instruct the reader without lecturing him** is better put as **Instruct the readers without lecturing them**. But some sentences cannot be satisfactorily rephrased in the plural: **Find a good teacher and take his advice** is not easily rendered gender-neutral. Avoid, above all, the sort of scrambled syntax that the Commission for Racial Equality had to adopt because it could not bring itself to use a singular pronoun: **We can't afford to squander anyone's talents, whatever colour their skin is.**

Avoid **chairperson** (chairwoman is permissible), **humankind** and **person in the street** – ugly expressions all. But remember that, in some contexts, the assumption that all people are men will be especially annoying just because it is wrong. **He will have to choose the best man for the job** is fine if you are talking about the pope selecting a bishop. If you are talking about Tony Blair appointing a new member of cabinet, it would be better to say **He will have to choose the best person for the job.**

Do not use words that make unwarranted assumptions about the sex of an interest group. Do you mean **housewives** or **consumers**, **mothers** or **parents**?

Refer to **women**, not **girls** (unless they are under 18) or **ladies**. If more women read *The Economist*, there would be fewer jobs for the boys.

SHORT WORDS. Use them. They are often Anglo-Saxon rather than Latin in origin. They are easy to spell and easy to understand. Thus prefer **about** to **approximately**, **after** to **following**, **let** to **permit**, **but** to **however**, **use** to **utilise**, **make** to **manufacture**, **plant** to **facility**, **take part** to **participate**, **set up** to **establish**, **enough** to **sufficient**, **show** to **demonstrate**, and so on. **Underdeveloped** countries are often better described as **poor**. **Substantive** usually means **real** or **big**.

SIMPLISTIC: prefer **simple-minded, naive**.

SKILLS. These are turning up all over the place – in learning skills, thinking skills, teaching skills – instead of **the ability to ... He has the skills** probably means **He can**.

SLANG. Do not be too free with **slang** (eg, **He really hit the big time in 1999**). Slang, like metaphors, should be used only occasionally if it is to have effect. Avoid expressions used only by journalists, such as giving people **the thumbs up, the thumbs down** or **the green light.** Stay clear of **gravy trains** and **salami tactics.** Do not use **the likes of** or **set to** (as in **profits being set to rise**). And avoid words or expressions that are ugly or overused, such as **aggressive, the bottom line, high profile, caring** (as an adjective), **carers, guesstimate** (use **guess**), **schizophrenic** (unless the context is medical), **crisis, hefty, key, major** (unless something else nearby is **minor**), **massive** (as in **massive inflation**), **meaningful, perceptions, prestigious** and **tough**.

Politicians are often said to be highly **visible**, when **conspicuous** would be more appropriate. Regulations are sometimes said to be designed to create **transparency**, which presumably means openness.

Try not to be predictable, especially not predictably jocular. Spare your readers any mention of **mandarins** when writing about the civil service and of **players** when you are talking about businessmen or women.

SMALL CAPITALS. Use small capitals for most abbreviations consisting of the first letter(s) of the abbreviated word(s). Exceptions are: currencies; degrees of temperature; some measures; and Latin words. See also ABBREVIATIONS.

SOME TIME means **at some point; sometime** means **former**.

SPECIFIC. A **specific** is a **medicine**, not a detail.

Spelling

Use British English rather than American English or any other kind (see also PART II). Sometimes, however, this injunction will clash with the rule that people and companies should be called what they want to be called, short of festooning themselves with titles. If it does, adopt American (or Canadian or other local) spelling when it is used in the name of an American (etc) company or private organisation (**Alcan Aluminum, Pulverizing Services Inc, Travelers Insurance**), but not when it is being used for a place or government institution (**Pearl Harbour, Department of Defence, Department of Labour**). The principle behind this ruling is that place names are habitually changed from foreign languages into English: **Deutschland** becomes **Germany**, **München Munich, Torino Turin**, etc. And to respect the local spelling of government institutions would present difficulties: a sentence containing both the **Department of Labor** and the **secretary of labour**, or the **Defense Department** and the **need for a strong defence**, would look unduly odd. That oddity will arise nonetheless if you have to explain that **Rockefeller Center Properties is in charge of Rockefeller Centre**, but with luck that will not happen too often.

The Australian **Labor Party** should be spelt without a u not only because it is not a government institution but also because the Australians spell it that way, although they spell **labour** as the British do.

Use **-ise, -isation** (**realise, organisation**) throughout. But please do not **hospitalise**.

Follow the preferences of companies or individuals themselves in writing their names.

For spelling rules for place names, see CITIES; COUNTRIES AND THEIR INHABITANTS; NAMES; PLACES; STATES, REGIONS, PROVINCES, COUNTIES.

For spelling rules for other proper names, see PEOPLE and COMPANIES. Other common difficulties are listed below (and see also -ABLE, -EABLE, -IBLE. See also PART II for American spellings.

Common problems

abattoir
accommodate
acknowledgment
acquittal
adviser, advisory
aeroplane, aircraft, airliner
aesthetic
Afrikaans (the language),
  Afrikaner (the person)

ageing (*but* caging, paging,
  raging, waging)
ambience
amid (*not* amidst)
amok (*not* amuck)
annex (verb), annexe (noun)
appal, appals, appalling,
  appalled
aqueduct

arbitrager
artefact
asinine
balk (*not* baulk)
balloted, balloting
bandwagon
benefited
biased
bicentenary (noun, *not* bicentennial)
billeted
blanketing
bogey (bogie is on a locomotive)
bolshie
born (given birth to), borne (carried)
borsch
braggadocio
bused, busing (keep bussing for kissing)
by-election, bylaw, bypass, by-product
bye (in sport only)
cannon (gun), canon (standard, criterion, clergyman)
canvas (cloth), canvass (seek opinion), canvassed
carcass
cashflow
caviare
chancy
channelled
checking account (spell it thus when explaining to Americans a current account, which is to be preferred)
choosy
cipher
clubable
combating
commemorate
complement (make complete), compliment (praise)

connection
consensus
coral (stuff found in sea), corral (cattle pen)
cosseted
council (assembly)
counsel (give advice)
defendant
dependant (person), dependent (adj)
depository (*unless* referring to American depositary receipts)
desiccation
detente (*not* détente)
dexterous (*not* dextrous)
discreet (prudent), discrete (separate)
disk (in a computer context), *otherwise* disc (including compact disc)
dispatch (*not* despatch)
dispel, dispelling
dissect
dissociate (*not* disassociate)
distil, distiller
divergences
douse (drench), dowse (use a divining rod)
dwelt
dyeing (colour)
dyke
ecstasy
embarrass (*but* harass)
encyclopedia
enroll, enrolment
ensure (make certain), insure (against risks)
enthrall
farther (distance), further (additional)
ferreted
fetid
fetus (*not* foetus, misformed

from the Latin *fetus*)
Filipino, Filipina (person),
  Philippine (adj of the
  Philippines)
filleted
flier, high-flier
flotation
focused, focusing
forbear (abstain),
  forebear (ancestor)
forbid (past tense forbade)
foreboding
foreclose
forefather
forestall
forewarn
forgather
forgo (do without),
  forego (precede)
forsake
forswear, forsworn
for ever (for all time),
  forever (unceasingly)
fuelled
-ful, *not* -full (armful,
  bathful, handful, etc)
fulfil, fulfilling
fullness
fulsome
gram (*not* gramme)
grey
grill (cook under flame)
grille (grating)
grisly (gruesome),
  grizzly (grey-haired;
  kind of bear)
guerrilla
gypsy
haemorrhage, haemorrhoids
hallo (*not* hello)
harass (*but* embarrass)
hiccup (*not* hiccough)
high-tech

hotch-potch
hurrah (*not* hooray)
hypocrisy, hypocrite
idiosyncrasy
idyll
impresario
inadvertent
incur, incurring
innocuous
inoculate
inquire, inquiry (*not* enquire,
  enquiry)
install, instalment, installation
instil, instilling
intransigent
jail (*not* gaol)
jewellery (*not* jewelry)
judgment
labelled
lacquer
laisser-faire
lama (priest), llama (beast)
lambast
leukaemia
levelled
liaise
libelled
licence (noun), license (verb)
lightening (making light),
  lightning (thunder and)
limited
linchpin, *but* lynch law
liquefy
liqueur (flavoured alcoholic
drink)
liquor (alcohol or other liquid)
literal (exact, factual, etc),
  littoral (shore)
loth (reluctant),
  loath (hate), loathsome
low-tech
manoeuvre (manoeuvring)
mantelpiece

marshal (noun and verb)
marshalled
mayonnaise
medieval
mêlée
meter (instrument for
  measuring),
  metre (linear measurement)
mileage
millennium (thousand years)
minuscule
modelled
mould
mouth (noun and verb)
mujahiddin
Muslim (*not* Moslem)
naivety
'Ndrangheta
nonplussed
nought (for numerals),
  otherwise naught
obbligato
occur, occurring
paediatric (-ian)
panel, panelled
parallel (-ed)
  paralleling
pastime
pedal (noun and verb,
  relating to foot lever)
peddle (to deal in trifles), *but*
  pedlar (not peddler)
peninsula (noun),
  peninsular (adj)
phoney (*not* phony)
piggyback (*not* pickaback)
plummeted
practice (noun), practise (verb)
predilection
preferred (-ing, *but* proffered)
preventive (*not* preventative)
principal (head; loan; or adj),
  principle (abstract noun)

privilege
proffered (-ing, *but* preferred)
profited
program (only in a computer
  context *otherwise* programme)
protester
pygmy
pzazz
questionnaire
queuing
rack (-ed, -ing, as in with pain,
  nerve-racking)
racket
rankle
rarefy
raze (*not* rase)
razzmattazz
recur, recurrent, recurring
refrigerator (*but* fridge)
regretted
renege
repairable (able to be repaired),
  reparable (of loss, able to be
  made good)
resemble, resemblance
restaurateur
resuscitate
rococo
rottweiler
saccharin (noun),
  saccharine (adj)
sacrilegious
salutary (remedial),
  salutatory (welcoming)
savannah
sceptic
seize
shaky
sheath (noun), sheathe (verb)
shibboleth
siege
sieve
skulduggery

smelt
smidgen (*not* smidgeon)
smoky
smooth (both noun and verb)
soothe
soyabean
specialty (*only* in context of medicine, steel and chemicals), *otherwise* speciality
sphinx
spoilt
stockmarket
storey (floor)
straits (narrow passage of water; position of difficulty)
straitjacket
straitlaced
stratagem
strategy
supersede
swap (*not* swop)
synonym
tariff
teetotalism, teetotaller
threshold
titbits
titillate

tormentor
trade union, trade unions (*but* Trades Union Congress)
transatlantic (*unless* trans-Pacific occurs close to it, when it must be trans-Atlantic)
transferred (-ing)
transsexual
travelled
tricolour
trouper (as in old trouper)
tsar
tyre
unparalleled
untrammelled
vaccinate
vacillate
visor
wagon (*not* waggon)
waive (to relinquish rights)
waver (to vacillate, tremble)
whisky (Scotch), whiskey (Irish)
wilful
withhold
wreath (noun), wreathe (verb)
wry, wrily

SPLIT INFINITIVES. To never split an infinitive is quite easy.

STATIONARY: still. **Stationery:** writing paper and so on.

STRAIGHT means **direct** or **uncurved**; **strait** means **narrow** or **tight**. The **strait-laced** tend to be **straight-faced**.

-STYLE. Avoid **German-style supervisory boards, an** EU**-style rotating presidency,** etc. Explain what you mean.

SUBCONTRACT. If you engage someone to do something, you are **contracting** the job to him; only if he then asks someone else to do it is the job **subcontracted**.

SUBJUNCTIVES. See INTRODUCTION, page 3; MAY AND MIGHT.

T

TABLE: avoid it as a transitive verb. In Britain to **table** means to bring something forward for action. In America it means the opposite.

TARGET is a noun, as is **trial**. If you are tempted to use **target** as a verb, try **aim** or **direct**. **Targeted** means **provided with a shield**.

THERE IS, THERE ARE: often unnecessary. **There were smiles on every face** is better as **A smile was on every face**. **There are three issues facing the prime minister** is better as **Three issues face the prime minister**.

TIMES: take care. **Three times more than x** means **four times as much as x**.

TITLES.
The overriding principle is to treat people with respect. That usually means giving them the title they themselves adopt. But some titles are misleading (all Italian graduates are Dr), and some tiresomely long (Mr Dr Dr Federal Sanitary-Inspector Schmidt). Do not indulge people's self-importance unless it would seem insulting not to.

Do not use Mr, Mrs, Miss, Ms or Dr on first mention even in body-matter. Plain **Bill Clinton, Tony Blair** or other appropriate combination of first name and surname will do. But thereafter for all living people drop the forename and use Mr, Mrs, Ms, Miss or some other title with the surname: **Jacques Chirac,** then **Mr Chirac. Governor X, President Y, the Rev John Z** may be **Mr, Mrs** or **Miss** on second mention. Knights, dames, lords, princes, kings, etc, should be given their title on first and subsequent mentions.

Titles are not necessary in headings or captions (surnames are; no Johns, Bills, etc). Sometimes they can also be dispensed with for athletes and rock stars, if titles would make them seem more ridiculous than dignified, and for criminals whose misdeeds are egregious. No titles for the dead, except those whom you are writing about because they have just died. **Dr Johnson** and **Mr Gladstone** are also permissible.

Take care with foreign titles. Malaysian ones are so confusing that it is wise to dispense with them altogether. Do not, however, call **Tunku Razaleigh Hamzah** Mr Razaleigh Hamzah; if you are not giving him his Tunku, refer to him, on each mention, as **Razaleigh Hamzah.** Avoid, above all, Mr Tunku Razaleigh Hamzah.

Use **Dr** only for qualified medical people, unless the correct alternative is not known or it would seem perverse to use **Mr.** And try to keep **Professor** for those who hold chairs, not just a university job or an inflated ego.

If you use a title, get it right. **Rear-Admiral** Jones should not, at least on first mention, be called **Admiral** Jones.

Life peeresses should be called **Lady,** not **Baroness,** just as barons are called **Lord.**

Avoid nicknames and diminutives unless the person is always known (or prefers to be known) by one: **Bill Emmott, Tony Blair, Bill Clinton, Newt Gingrich.**

Avoid the habit of joining office and name: **Prime Minister Blair, Budget Commissioner Liikanen;** but **Chancellor Schröder** is permissible.

Omit middle initials. Nobody will imagine that the **Lyndon Johnson** you are writing about is **Lyndon A. Johnson** or **Lyndon C. Johnson.**

The title **Ms,** which was created to provide a female equivalent for the all-purpose male title **Mr,** is permissible though ugly. Married women who are known by their maiden names – eg, Aung San Suu Kyi, Benazir Bhutto, Jane Fonda – are **Miss** unless they have made it clear that they want to be called something else. Whenever possible, find out which title the woman herself prefers.

Some titles serve as names, and therefore have initial capitals, though they also serve as descriptions: **the Archbishop of Canterbury, the Emir of Kuwait.** If you want to describe the office rather than the individual, use lower case: **The next archbishop of Canterbury will be a woman.** Use lower case, too, in references simply to **the duke, the emir, the shah: The Duchess of Scunthorpe was in her finery, but the duke wore jeans.**

TOTAL: all right as a noun, but as a verb prefer **amount to** or **add up to.**

TRANSPIRE means **exhale,** not **happen, occur** or **turn out.**

U

UNIQUE means **the only one of its kind** and cannot be qualified; it is nonsense to describe something as **almost/rather/the most unique.**

UNLIKE should not be followed by **in.** See LIKE.

UNNECESSARY WORDS. Some words add nothing but length to your prose. Use adjectives to make your meaning more precise and be cautious of those you find yourself using to make it more emphatic. The word **very** is a case in point. If it occurs in a sentence you have written, try leaving it out. **The omens were good** may have more force than **The omens were very good.**

Avoid **strike action** (**strike** will do), **cutbacks** (**cuts**), **track record** (**record**), **wilderness area** (usually either a **wilderness** or a **wild area**), **large-scale** (**big**), **weather conditions** (**weather**), etc.

Shoot off, or rather shoot, as many prepositions after verbs as possible. Thus people can **meet** rather than **meet with**; companies can be **bought** and **sold** rather than **bought up** and **sold off**; budgets can be **cut** rather than **cut back**; plots can be **hatched** but not **hatched up**; organisations should be **headed** by rather than **headed up** by chairmen just as markets should be **freed**, rather than **freed up**. And children can be **sent** to bed rather than **sent off** to bed.

The word **community** is usually unnecessary. So the **black community** means **blacks**, the **business community** means **business**, the **homosexual community** means **homosexuals**, the **international community**, if it means anything, means **other countries, aid agencies** or, just occasionally, **the family of nations.**

Use words with care. A **heart condition** is usually a **bad heart. Positive thoughts** presumably means **optimism**, just as a **negative report** is probably a **critical report. Industrial action** is usually **industrial inaction, industrial disruption** or **strike**. A **substantially finished** bridge is an **unfinished** bridge, a **major speech** usually just a **speech.** Something with **reliability problems** probably **does not work.** If yours is a **live audience**, what would a dead one be like?

USE AND ABUSE: two words much used and abused. You **take** drugs, not **use** them (Does he use sugar?). And **drug abuse** is just **drug taking**, as is **substance abuse**, unless it is **glue sniffing** or **bun throwing.**

V • W

VENAL. In some countries, petty officials are **venal** – that is, open to bribery. But, when you consider how little they are paid, you may count it a **venial** – that is, pardonable – sin.

VENERABLE means **worthy of reverence.** It is not a synonym for **old.**

VENUES: avoid them. Try **places.**

VERBAL. Every agreement, except the nod-and-wink variety, is **verbal.** If you mean one that was not written down, describe it as **oral.**

VIABLE means **capable of living.** Do not apply it to things like railway lines. **Economically viable** means **profitable.**

•

WARN is transitive, so you must either **give warning** or **warn somebody.**

WHEREABOUTS are plural.

WHICH informs, **that** defines. **This is the house that Jack built.** But **This house, which Jack built, is now falling down.**

WHILE (not **whilst**) is best used temporally. Do not use it in place of **although** or **whereas.**

PART II

AMERICAN AND BRITISH ENGLISH

The differences between English as written and spoken in America and English as used in Britain are considerable, as is the potential for misunderstanding, even offence, when using words or phrases that are unfamiliar or mean something else on the other side of the Atlantic. This section highlights the important differences of American and British English spelling, grammar and usage.

VOCABULARY. Sometimes the same word has taken on different meanings on the two sides of the Atlantic, creating an opportunity for misunderstanding. The word **homely**, for example, means **simple** or **informal** in British English, but **plain** or **unattractive** in American English.

This also applies to figures of speech. **It went like a bomb** in British English means it was a great success; **it bombed** in American English means it was a disaster. **To table** something in British English means to bring it forward for action; but in American English it means the opposite.

EXCLUSIVITY. What is familiar in one culture may be entirely alien in another. British English exploits terms and phrases borrowed from the game of cricket; American English uses baseball terms. Anyone writing for readers in both markets uses either set of terms at their peril. Do not make references or assumptions that are geographically exclusive, for example by specifying months when referring to seasonal patterns, by using north or south to imply a type of climate, or by making geographical references that give state name followed by USA, as in Wyoming, USA.

One writer's slang is another's lively use of words; formal language to one is pomposity to another. This is the trickiest area to negotiate when writing for both British and American readers. At its best, distinctively American English is more direct and vivid than its British English equivalent. Many American words and expressions have passed into British English because they are shorter or more to the point: phrases like **lay off**, preferable to **make redundant**. But American English also has a contrary tendency to lengthen words, creating a (to British readers) pompous tone: for instance, **transportation** (in British English, **transport**).

British English is slower than American English to accept new words, and suspicious of short cuts. In particular, it resists the use as verbs of nouns such as **author, critique, host, impact, haemorrhage, loan, party, pressure** and **roundtable**. American English, however, does not like some perfectly good words – **sufficient** is almost always **enough** and **comprise** becomes **contain, include** or **is made up of**. American

English is also fast to adopt new usages for words such as **scenario, posture, parameter.**

SYNTAX AND SENTENCE STRUCTURE. American English may also use different syntax and sentence construction. Written American English tends to be more declarative than its British counterpart, and adverbs and some modifying phrases are frequently positioned differently. For example, British English may say, **"As well as going shopping, we went to the park."** American English would turn the opening phrase around: **"We went to the park as well as going shopping"**, or would begin the sentence with **"In addition to"**. British English also tends to use more compound modifying phrases, while American English prefers to go with simpler sentence structure.

In British English doctors and lawyers are to be found **in** Harley Street or Wall Street, not **on** it. And they rest from their labours **at** weekends, not **on** them. During the week their children are **at** school, not **in** it.

Words may also be inserted or omitted in some standard phrases. British English goes **to hospital**, American English **to the hospital**. British English chooses between **one or other thing**; American English chooses **one thing or the other.**

SPELLING. Some words are spelt differently; the spellings are sufficiently similar to identify the word, but the unfamiliar form may still disturb the reader. It may be better to use a synonym than to take this risk, although sometimes it cannot be avoided.

SPECIAL PROBLEMS. A number of subjects call for highly detailed, specialised guidance beyond the scope of this book, though some of the vocabulary is dealt with here. These areas include food and cookery (different names for ingredients and equipment; different systems of measurement); medicine and health care (different professional titles, drug names, therapies); human anatomy (different attitudes to the depiction of sexual organs); and gardening (different seasons and plants). Many crafts and hobbies also use different terms for equipment, materials and techniques.

RACE AND SEX. The difficulties that arise in Europe with references to race and sex (see ETHNIC GROUPS, SEXISM) are even greater in America where readers are often more sensitive. When referring to Americans whose ancestors came from Africa, many people are using **African-American** rather than **black**. It is totally unacceptable to refer to **American Indians** as **red**. It can also cause offence to describe the original inhabitants of the lands stretching from Greenland to Alaska as **Eskimos;**

this was a corruption of a Cree word meaning **raw flesh eater.** The people themselves have at least three major tribal groupings. **Alaska natives** are usually called **native Americans** in Alaska. **Inuit** should only be used to refer to people from that tribe.

It is unwise to describe an adult American female as a **girl.**

A joint dictionary

USE -IZE, NOT -ISE. The American convention is to spell with **z** many words that some British writers (including *The Economist*) spell with **s.** Few British readers object to this. Remember, though, that some words must end in **-ise,** whichever spelling convention is being followed. These include:

advertise	despise	incise
advise	devise	merchandise
apprise	disguise	premise
arise	emprise	prise
chastise	enfranchise	revise
circumcise	excise	supervise
comprise	exercise	surmise
compromise	franchise	surprise
demise	improvise	televise

Note that words with the ending **-lyse,** such as **analyse** and **paralyse,** should not be spelt **-lyze** in British English, even though they are commonly spelt thus in American English.

WORDS GENERALLY ACCEPTABLE IN BOTH BRITISH AND AMERICAN ENGLISH.

ambience *not* ambiance
among *not* amongst
annex *not* annexe
artifact *not* artefact
backward *not* backwards
baptistry *not* baptistery
Bible *not* bible
Bordeaux *not* claret, for red wine of region
burned *not* burnt
bus *not* coach
busy *not* engaged, for telephones

canvases *not* canvasses
car rental *not* car hire
carryall *not* holdall
cater to *not* cater for
custom-made *not* bespoke
day nursery *not* crèche
development *not* estate, for housing
diesel fuel *not* derv
disc *not* disk, except in computing
dispatch *not* despatch

encyclopedia *not* encyclopaedia
except for *not* save
farther *not* further, for distance
first name *not* Christian name
flashlight *not* torch
flip *not* toss, for coin, etc
focusing, focused, etc
fuel *not* petrol (UK) or gasoline (US)
forward *not* forwards
(eye)glasses *not* spectacles
grille *not* grill, for grating
gypsy *not* gipsy
hairdryer *not* hairdrier
horse-racing *not just* racing
inquire *not* enquire
insurance coverage *not* insurance cover
intermission *not* interval
jail *not* gaol
learned *not* learnt
like *not* fancy
line *not* queue
located *not* situated
location *not* situation
maid *not* chambermaid
mathematics *not* maths (UK) or math (US)
merry-go-round *not* roundabout
motorcycle *not* motorbike
neat *not* spruce or tidy
newsstand *not* kiosk
nightgown *not* nightdress
okra *not* lady's fingers
onto *not* on to
orangeade/lemonade *not* orange/lemon squash
package *not* parcel
parking spaces/garage *not* car park (UK) or parking lot (US)
pharmacy *not* chemist (UK) or drugstore (US)

phoney *not* phony
priority *not* right of way, for vehicles
refrigerator *not* fridge
railway station *not* railroad station
raincoat *not* mac, mackintosh
rent *not* hire, except for people
reservation, reserve (seats, etc) *not* booking, book
retired person *not* old-age pensioner (UK) or retiree (US)
sanatorium *not* sanitarium
slowdown *not* go-slow, in production
soccer *not* football, except for American football
sorbet *not* water-ice (UK) or sherbet (US)
spelled *not* spelt
spoiled *not* spoilt
street musician *not* busker
swap *not* swop
swimming *not* bathing
team *not* side, in sport
tearoom *not* teashop
thread *not* cotton
toilet *not* lavatory
toll-free *not* free of charge
trainers *not* plimsolls (UK) or sneakers (US)
tuna *not* tunny
underwear *not* pants or knickers; or use lingerie for women's underwear
unmistakable *not* unmistakeable
unspoiled *not* unspoilt
while *not* whilst
whimsy, whimsies *not* whimsey, whimseys
workman *not* navvy
yogurt *not* yoghourt or yoghurt

Problematic words and phrases

DIFFERENT SPELLING CONVENTIONS.
American English is more obviously phonetic than British English. The word **cosy** becomes **cozy**, **aesthetic** becomes **esthetic**, **sizeable** becomes **sizable**, **arbour** becomes **arbor**, **theatre** becomes **theater**, **draught** becomes **draft**.
The main spelling differences between American English and British English are as follows.

-eable/-able. The silent **e**, created when forming some adjectives with this suffix, is more often omitted in American English; thus, **likeable** is spelt **likable, unshakeable** is spelt **unshakable**. But the **e** is sometimes retained in American English where it affects the sound of the preceding consonant; thus, **traceable**, or **manageable**.

-ae/-oe. Although it is now common in British English to write **medieval** rather than **mediaeval**, other words – often scientific terms such as **aeon, diarrhoea, anaesthetic, gynaecology, homoeopathy** – retain their classical composite vowel. In American English, the composite vowel is replaced by a single **e**; thus, **eon, diarrhea, anesthetic, gynecology, homeopathy**.

-ce/-se. In British English, the verb that relates to a noun ending in **-ce** is sometimes given the ending **-se**; thus, **advice** (noun), **advise** (verb), **device/devise, licence/license, practice/practise**. In the first two instances, the spelling change is accompanied by a slight change in the sound of the word; but in the other two instances, noun and verb are pronounced the same way, and American English spelling reflects this, by using the same spelling: thus, **license** and **practice**. It also extends the use of **-se** to other nouns which in British English are spelt **-ce**: thus, **defense, offense, pretense**.

-e/-ue. The final silent **e** or **ue** of several words is omitted in American English but retained in British English: thus, **analog/ analogue, ax/axe, catalog/catalogue**.

-ll/-l. In British English, when words ending in the consonant l are given a suffix beginning with a vowel (eg, the suffixes **-able, -ed, -ing, -ous, -y**), the l is doubled; thus, **annul/annulled, model/modelling, quarrel/quarrelling, rebel/rebellious, wool/woolly**. This is inconsistent with the general rule in British English that the final consonant is doubled before the suffix only when the preceding vowel carries the main stress: thus, the word **regret** becomes **regretted**, or **regrettable**; but the word **billet** becomes **billeted**. American English mostly does not have this inconsistency. So if the stress does not fall on the preceding vowel, the l is not doubled: thus, **model/modeling, travel/traveler**; but **annul/annulled**.

Several words which end in a single l in British English – eg, **appal, fulfil** – take a double ll in American English. In British English, the l stays single when the word takes a suffix beginning with a consonant (eg, the suffixes -ful, -fully, -ment): thus, **fulfil/ fulfilment**. Moreover, words ending in -ll usually lose one l when taking one of these suffixes: thus, **skill/skilful, will/wilfully**. In American English, words ending in -ll usually remain intact, whatever the suffix: thus, **skill/skillful, will/willfully**.

-our/-or. Most British English words ending in -our – **ardour, behaviour, candour, demeanour, favour, valour** and the like – lose the **u** in American English: thus, **ardor, candor**, etc. The major exception is **glamour**, which retains its **u**.

-re/-er. Most British English words ending in -re – such as **centre, fibre, metre, theatre** – end in -er in American English: thus, **center, fiber**, etc. Exceptions include: **acre, cadre, lucre, massacre, mediocre, ogre**.

-t/-ed (past tense). British English uses -t – **spelt, learnt, burnt** – whereas American English uses -ed – **spelled, learned, burned**.

HYPHENATION.
American English is far readier than British English to accept compound words. In particular, many nouns made of two separate nouns are spelt as one word in American English, while in British English they would either remain separate or be joined by a hyphen: eg, **applesauce** (hyphenated in British English). British English also tends, more than American English, to use hyphens as pronunciation aids or to separate identical letters in words such as **co-operation, pre-empt, re-examine**.

American English likes hyphenated adjectives such as **in-depth, in-flight**, which although common in British English are deprecated.

COMMON PROBLEMATIC WORDS.
The following list draws attention to commonly used words and idioms that either are spelt differently or have different meanings in American English and British English. It does not cover slang or colloquialisms.

If you want to produce a single version of written material which will be acceptable to both sorts of readers, you should avoid using the words in this list when there is a mutually acceptable alternative (see pages 78–79). If not, follow one or other convention, and, if this means using a word that will mystify or mislead one group of readers, provide a translation.

British	American
accommodation (lodging/s)	accommodation/s (lodging/s)
adopt (a candidate)	nominate
aerial (TV)	antenna
air hostess	flight attendant
aluminium	aluminum
anti-clockwise	counterclockwise
apophthegm	apothegm
apple purée	applesauce
at weekends	on weekends
aubergine	eggplant
autumn	fall
baby's dummy	pacifier
baking tray	baking sheet
bag, handbag	purse, pocketbook
banknote	bill
barrister	trial lawyer
behove	behoove
bicarbonate of soda	baking soda
bilberry	blueberry
bill	check
biscuit (sweet)	cookie
biscuit (savoury)	cracker
black treacle	molasses
blind (for windows)	shade
bowler (hat)	derby
braces	suspenders
building society	savings and loan association
calibre	caliber
camp bed	cot
car, estate	station wagon
car, saloon	sedan
car bonnet	hood
car boot	trunk
car demister	defogger

British	American
car dipswitch	dimmer
car jump leads	jumper cables
car park	parking lot
car silencer	muffler
car windscreen	windshield
car wing	fender
caravan	house trailer
cheque (bank)	check
chequered	checkered (pattern)
chickpea	garbanzo bean (and chickpea)
chilli/chillies	chili/chilis
chips	French fries
choux bun	cream puff
cinema	movie theater
clever	smart
cling film	plastic wrap
coach	bus
coriander (fresh)	cilantro
corn	wheat
cornflour	cornstarch
cosy	cozy
cot	crib
country	nation
courgette	zucchini
crayfish	crawfish
crisps	chips
crossroads/junction	intersection
crystallised	candied
cupboard/wardrobe	closet
demerara sugar	light-brown sugar
desiccated coconut	shredded coconut
dialled	dialed
diary (appointments)	calendar
diary (record)	journal
digestive biscuit	graham cracker
district	neighborhood
double cream	heavy cream
draught	draft
dressing gown	bathrobe/housecoat
drug (hard drug)	narcotic
dual carriageway	four-lane (or divided) highway
dyke	dike

British	American
essence (eg, vanilla)	extract or flavoring
estate agent	realtor/real estate agent
ex-serviceman	veteran
eyrie	aerie
flan tin	pie plate
flat	apartment
fillet (boneless meat/fish)	filet
flour, plain	flour, all-purpose
flour, self-raising	flour, self-rising
flour, wholemeal	flour, whole-wheat
flyover	overpass
from ... to ...	through
frying pan	skillet (or frying pan)
fuelled	fueled
full stop (punctuation)	period, stop
furore	furor
give way	yield
golden syrup	corn syrup
greengrocer's	vegetable market
grey	gray
grill (verb and noun)	broil (verb), broiler (noun)
ground floor	first floor
high street	main street
hire (of car)	rent or hire
holiday	vacation (but public holiday)
home from home	home away from home
homely	homey/homy (homely = plain)
icing sugar	powdered or confectioners' sugar
in (Fifth Avenue, etc)	on
increase (of money)	hike
jeweller/jewellery	jeweler/jewelry
jumper	sweater
kerb/kerbside	curb/curbside
ketchup	catsup
labelled	labeled
ladder (in stocking)	run
lawyer	attorney (or lawyer)
lease of life	lease on life
lent	loaned
lift	elevator
liquidiser	blender
lorry	truck

British	American
lustre	luster
maize/sweetcorn	corn
manoeuvre/manoeuvrable	maneuver/maneuverable
mean (parsimonious)	stingy, tight (mean = nasty)
meet	meet with
metre (unit of distance)	meter
minced meat	ground meat
modelled	modeled
motor-racing	auto-racing
motorway	superhighway, freeway, expressway
mould/moulder/moult	mold/molder/molt
moustache	mustache
mum/mummy	mom/mommy
muslin	cheesecloth
nappy	diaper
nervy	nervous (nervy = brazen)
oblige	obligate
omelette	omelet
ordinary	regular, normal
outside	outside of
paddling pool	wading pool
panelled	wood-paneled
pants	underpants
pastry case	pie crust
pavement	sidewalk
pepper (red, green, etc)	sweet pepper or pepper
petrol	gasoline, gas
petrol station	gas/service station
pips	seeds (in fruit)
pitta bread	pita bread
plain/dark chocolate	semisweet or unsweetened chocolate
plait	braid
plough	plow
podgy	pudgy
polythene	polyethylene
post, post box	mail, mailbox
power point	electrical outlet
pram, push chair	stroller
programme (except computer)	program
property (land)	real estate

British	American
pumpkin	squash
pyjamas	pajamas
queue	line, line up
quitted (past tense and participle of quit)	quit
rambler	hiker
rationalisation (personnel)	downsizing
removal van	moving van
riding (horses)	horseback riding
ring road	beltway
rivalled	rivaled
rowing boat	rowboat
run in (car, engine)	break in
scallywag	scalawag
sceptical	skeptical
senior	ranking (political)
shortcrust pastry	pie dough
shorthand typist	stenographer
single cream	light cream
sizeable	sizable
skilful	skillful
sleepers	railroad ties
smoulder	smolder
soda water	seltzer
solicitor	attorney
sombre	somber
soya	soy
spanner	wrench
specialist shop	specialty shop
speciality (but specialty for medicine, steel and chemicals)	specialty
sponge finger biscuits	ladyfingers
spring onion	scallion
stand (for election)	run
stocks	inventory
stone	rock
stoned (cherries, etc)	pitted
storey (of building)	story
stupid	dumb
subway	pedestrian underpass
sulphur(ous)	sulfur(ous)

British	*American*
sultana	golden (seedless) raisin
sweated (past tense and participle of sweat)	sweat
sweet shop	candy store
tap	faucet
terraced house	row house
till	check-out
titbit	tidbit
towards	toward
transport	transportation
trainers	sneakers
traveller/travelled	traveler/traveled
trousers	pants or slacks (trousers acceptable)
trunk call	long-distance call
turning (road)	turnoff
tyre	tire
underground (or tube train)	subway
upmarket	upscale
vest	undershirt
waistcoat	vest
walk	hike (only if more energetic than a walk)
water biscuit	cracker
way out	exit
woollen/woolly	woolen/wooly
work out (problem)	figure out
zip	zipper

Differences in punctuation

COMMA IN LISTS. Americans often put a comma before the **and: eggs, bacon, potatoes, and cheese.** The British more often write **eggs, bacon, potatoes and cheese.**

DASHES. In British publications, the usual style for a dash used as a parenthesis is an en-rule (–) with a character space either side. In American publications – and *The Economist* newspaper – the usual style for a dash is an em-rule (—) with no spaces.

FULL STOPS (PERIODS). The American convention is to use full stops (periods) to identify almost all abbreviations. The British convention is to keep them to a minimum.

QUOTATION MARKS. In American publications (and those of major Commonwealth countries), the convention is to use double quotation marks, reserving single quotation marks for quotes within quotes. In British publications, the convention is the reverse (except in *The Economist*): single quotation marks are used first, then double. However, the American style is becoming more popular.

The relative position of quotation marks and other punctuation is far more contentious. The British convention is to place such punctuation according to sense. The American convention is simpler but less logical: all commas and full stops precede the final quotation mark (or, if there is a quote within a quote, the first final quotation mark). Other punctuation – colons, semi-colons, question and exclamation marks – is placed according to sense. The following examples illustrate the differences.

American style

The words on the magazine's cover, "The link between coffee and cholesterol," caught his eye.

"You're eating too much," she told him. "You'll soon look like your father."

"Have you seen this article, 'The link between coffee and cholesterol'?" he asked.

"It was as if," he explained, "I had swallowed a toad, and it kept croaking 'ribbut, ribbut,' from deep in my stomach."
She particularly enjoyed the article "Looking for the 'New Man.' "

British style
The words on the magazine's cover, 'The link between coffee and cholesterol', caught his eye.
'Have you seen this article, "The link between coffee and cholesterol"?' he asked.
'You're eating too much,' she told him. 'You'll soon look like your father.'
'It was as if,' he explained, 'I had swallowed a toad, and it kept croaking "ribbut, ribbut", from deep in my belly.'
She particularly enjoyed the article 'Looking for the "New Man" '.

Different units of measurement

In British publications measurements are now largely expressed in SI units (the modern form of metric units), although imperial measures are still used in certain contexts. In American publications measurements may be expressed in SI or imperial units.

Although in most cases the British imperial and American standard measures are identical, there are some important exceptions. There are also some measures peculiar to one or other national system, particularly units of mass relating to agriculture. See also MEASUREMENTS (Part I) and MEASURES (Part III).

PART III

FACT CHECKER AND GLOSSARY

A

ABBREVIATIONS.

Here is a list of some common business abbreviations. See also AB-
BREVIATIONS, pages 6–7.

AG	*Aktiengesellschaft* (German or Swiss public limited company)
AGM	annual general meeting
AIM	Alternative Investment Market (UK)
APR	annual percentage rate
ASSC	Accounting Standards Steering Committee (UK)
CAPM	capital asset pricing model
CCA	current cost accounting
CEO	chief executive officer
CFO	chief financial officer
CGT	capital gains tax
cif	cost, insurance, freight
COB	Commission des Opérations de Bourse (Stock Exchange Commission, France)
Consob	Commissione Nazionale per le Società e la Borsa (Stock Exchange Commission, Italy)
COO	chief operating officer
COSA	cost of sales adjustment
CPA	certified public accountant (USA); critical path analysis
CPP	current purchasing power (accounting)
DCF	discounted cash flow
EFT	electronic funds transfer
EFTPOS	electronic funds transfer at point of sale
EMS	European Monetary System
EMU	economic and monetary union
EPS	earnings per share
EU	European Union
FASB	Financial Accounting Standards Board (USA)
FIFO	first in, first out (used for valuing stock/inventory)
fob	free on board
forex	foreign exchange
FSA	Financial Services Authority (UK)
GAAP	generally accepted accounting principles (USA)
GmbH	*Gesellschaft mit beschränkter Haftung* (German or Swiss private limited company)
IRR	internal rate of return
IRS	Internal Revenue Service (USA)
LIFFE	London International Financial Futures Exchange

LIFO	last in, first out (used for valuing stock/inventory value, popular in USA)
M&A	mergers and acquisitions
MCT	mainstream corporation tax
MLR	minimum lending rate
NASDAQ	National Association of Securities Dealers Automated Quotations System (USA)
NBV	net book value
NPV	net present value; no par value
NRV	net realisable value
NYSE	New York Stock Exchange
Nymex	New York Mercantile Exchange
NRV	net realisable value
P/E	price/earnings ratio
P&L a/c	profit and loss account (known as the income statement in the USA)
PLC	public limited company (UK)
PSBR	public-sector borrowing rate
R&D	research and development
ROA	return on assets
ROCE	return on capital employed
ROE	return on equity
ROI	return on investment
ROOA	return on operating assets
ROTA	return on total assets
SA	*société anonyme* (French, Belgian, Luxembourg or Swiss public limited company)
Sarl	*société à responsabilité limitée* (French, etc private limited company)
SEAQ	Stock Exchange Automated Quotation System (UK)
SEC	Securities and Exchange Commission (USA)
SITC	standard international trade classification
SRO	self-regulating organisation
SSAP	Statement of Standard Accounting Practice (UK)
UEC	Union Européenne des Experts Comptables Economiques et Financiers
VAT	value-added tax
ZBB	zero base budgeting

For international bodies and their abbreviations, see ORGANISATIONS, pages 130ff.

ACCENTS. Here are some of the more familiar foreign-language accents.

acute   république
grave   grand'mère
circumflex   bête noire
umlaut   Länder, Österreich (Austria)
cedilla   français
tilde   señor, São Paulo

ACCOUNTANCY RATIOS.
These are the ratios most commonly used in accounting practice.

Working capital

Working capital ratio = current assets/current liabilities, where current assets = stock + debtors + cash at bank and in hand + quoted investments, etc, current liabilities = creditors + overdraft at bank + taxation + dividends, etc. The ratio varies according to type of trade and conditions; a ratio from 1 to 3 is usual with a ratio above 2 being generally good.

Liquidity ratio = liquid ("quick") assets/current liabilities, where liquid assets = debtors + cash at bank and in hand + quoted investments (that is assets which can be realised within a month or so, which may not apply to all investments); current liabilities are those which may need to be repaid within the same short period, which may not necessarily include a bank overdraft where it is likely to be renewed. The liquidity ratio is sometimes referred to as the "acid test"; a ratio under 1 suggests a possibly difficult situation, while too high a ratio may mean that assets are not being usefully employed.

Turnover of working capital = sales/average working capital. The ratio varies according to type of trade; generally a low ratio can mean poor use of resources, while too high a ratio can mean over-trading.

Turnover of stock = sales/average stock, or (where cost of sales is known) = cost of sales/average stock. The cost of sales turnover figure is to be preferred as both figures are then on the same valuation basis. This ratio can be expressed as number of times per year, or time taken for stock to be turned over once = (52/number of times) weeks. A low turnover of stock can be a sign of stocks which are difficult to move, and is usually a sign of adverse conditions.

Turnover of debtors = credit sales/average debtors. This indicates efficiency in collecting accounts. An average "credit period" of about one month is usual, but varies according to credit stringency conditions in the economy.

Turnover of creditors = purchases/average creditors. Average payment period is best maintained in line with turnover of debtors.

Sales
Export ratio = exports as a percentage of sales.
Sales per employee = sales/average number of employees.

Assets
Ratios of assets can vary according to the measure of assets used:
Total assets = current assets + fixed assets + other assets, where fixed assets = property + plant and machinery + motor vehicles, etc, and other assets = long-term investment + goodwill, etc.
Net assets ("net worth") = total assets - total liabilities
$$= \text{share capital + reserves}$$
Turnover of net assets = sales/average net assets. As for turnover of working capital, a low ratio can mean poor use of resources.
Assets per employee = assets/average number of employees. Indicates the amount of investment backing for employees.

Profits
Profit margin = (profit/sales) × 100 = profits as a percentage of sales; usually profits before tax.
Profitability = (profit/total assets) × 100 = profits as a percentage of total assets.
Return on capital = (profit/net assets) × 100 = profits as a percentage of net assets ("net worth" or "capital employed").

B

BEAUFORT SCALE. The Beaufort Scale, once a picturesque fleet of well-scrubbed men-o'-war and fishing smacks, has been rendered bland by the World Meteorological Organization.

The Beaufort Scale

Conditions (abbreviated)				Equivalent speed at 10m height		
Force	Description	On land	At sea	knots	miles per hour	metres per second
0	Calm	Smoke rises vertically	Sea like a mirror	less than 1	less than 1	0.0–0.2
1	Light air	Smoke drifts	Ripples	1–3	1–3	0.3–1.5
2	Light breeze	Leaves rustle	Small wavelets	4–6	4–7	1.7–3.3
3	Gentle breeze	Wind extends light flag	Large wavelets, crests break	7–10	8–12	3.4–5.4
4	Moderate breeze	Raises paper and dust	Small waves, some white horses	11–16	13–18	5.5–7.9
5	Fresh breeze	Small trees in leaf sway	Moderate waves, many white horses	17–21	19–24	8.0–10.7
6	Strong breeze	Large branches in motion	Large waves form, some spray	22–27	25–31	10.8–13.8
7	Moderate gale or near gale	Whole trees in motion	Sea heaps up, white foam streaks	28–33	32–38	13.9–17.1
8	Fresh gale or gale	Breaks twigs off trees	Moderately high waves, well-marked foam streaks	34–40	39–46	17.2–20.7
9	Strong gale	Slight structural damage to tumble over	High waves, crests start	41–47	47–54	20.8–24.4
10	Whole gale or storm	Trees uprooted, considerable structural damage	Very high waves, white sea tumbles	48–55	55–63	24.5–28.4
11	Storm or violent storm	Very rarely experienced, widespread damage	Exceptionally high waves, edges of wave crests blown to froth	56–63	64–72	28.5–32.6
12–17	Hurricane	Devastation with driving spray	Sea completely white	64–118	73–136	32.7–over

C

CALENDARS.

There are six important solar calendars.

Gregorian	Iranian[b]	Hindu[c]
January (31)[a]		
February (28 or 29)		
March (31)	Favardin (31)	Caitra (30)
April (30)	Ordibehesht (31)	Vaisakha (31)
May (31)	Khordad (31)	Jyaistha (31)
June (30)	Tir (31)	Asadha (31)
July (31)	Mordad (31)	Sravana (31)
August (31)	Sharivar (31)	Bhadrapada (31)
September (30)	Mehr (30)	Asvina (30)
October (31)	Aban (30)	Karttika (30)
November (30)	Azar (30)	Margasirsa (30)
December (31)	Dey (30)	Pausa (30)
(January)	Bahman (30)	Magha (30)
(February)	Esfand (28 or 29)	Phalguna (30)

Gregorian	Ethiopian[d]	Jewish[e]
September (30)	Maskerem (30)	Tishri (30)
October (31)	Tikimit (30)	Cheshvan (29 or 30)
November (30)	Hidar (30)	Kislev (29 or 30)
December (31)	Tahsas (30)	Tebet (29)
(January)	Tir (30)	Shebat (30)
(February)	Yekatit (30)	Adar (29)
(March)	Megabit (30)	Nisan (30)
(April)	Miazia (30)	Iyyar (29)
(May)	Guenbot (30)	Sivan (30)
(June)	Sene (30)	Tammuz (29)
(July)	Hamle (30)	Ab (30)
(August)	Nahassie (30+5 or 6)	Elul (29)

a Figures in brackets denote the number of days in that month.
b Months begin about the 21st of the corresponding Gregorian month.
c Months begin about the 22nd of the corresponding Gregorian month.
d Months begin on the 11th of the corresponding Gregorian month.
e The date of the new year varies, but normally falls in the second half of September in the Gregorian calendar; the general calendar position is maintained by adding, in some years, an extra period of 29 days, Adar Sheni, following the month of Adar.

The Muslim calendar. Muslims use a lunar calendar which begins 10 or 11 days earlier each year in terms of the Gregorian. The months, whose names follow, do not have a fixed number of days.

Muharram	Rajab
Safar	Shaaban
Rabia I	Ramadan
Rabia II	Shawwal
Jumada I	Dhu al-Kadah
Jumada II	Dhu al-Hijjah

In each 30 years, 19 years have 354 days (are "common") and 11 have 355 days (are "intercalary").

The Muslim years in the left-hand column below began on the dates of the Gregorian calendar as shown.

1411	July 24th 1990	1417	May 19th 1996
1412	July 13th 1991	1418	May 9th 1997
1413	July 2nd 1992	1419	April 28th 1998
1414	June 21st 1993	1420	April 17th 1999
1415	June 9th 1994	1421	April 6th 2000
1416	May 31st 1995	1422	March 26th 2001

CARS.

Here is a list of some international vehicle registration (IVR) letters.

A	Austria	CI	Côte d'Ivoire
AL	Albania	CL	Sri Lanka
AND	Andorra	CO	Colombia
AO	Angola	CR	Costa Rica
ARM	Armenia	CY	Cyprus
AUS	Australia	CZ	Czech Republic
B	Belgium	D	Germany
BD	Bangladesh	DK	Denmark
BDS	Barbados	DOM	Dominican Republic
BG	Bulgaria	DZ	Algeria
BIH	Bosnia & Hercegovina	E	Spain
BOL	Bolivia	EAK	Kenya
BR	Brazil	EAU	Uganda
BW	Botswana	EC	Ecuador
CAM	Cameroon	ES	El Salvador
CDN	Canada	EST	Estonia
CH	Switzerland	ET	Egypt

F	France	NZ	New Zealand
FIN	Finland	P	Portugal
FL	Liechtenstein	PE	Peru
GB	Great Britain	PK	Pakistan
GBG	Guernsey	PL	Poland
GBJ	Jersey	PY	Paraguay
GBZ	Gibraltar	QA	Qatar
GE	Georgia	RA	Argentina
GR	Greece	RC	China
H	Hungary	RCH	Chile
HK	Hong Kong	RI	Indonesia
HKJ/JOR	Jordan	RL	Lebanon
HR	Croatia	RO	Romania
I	Italy	ROK	South Korea
IL	Israel	ROU	Uruguay
IND	India	RP	Philippines
IR	Iran	RSM	San Marino
IRL	Ireland	RUS	Russia
IRQ	Iraq	RV	Burundi
IS	Iceland	S	Sweden
J	Japan	SA	Saudi Arabia
KG	Kirgizstan	SG	Singapore
KWT	Kuwait	SK	Slovakia
KZ	Kazakhstan	SLO	Slovenia
L	Luxembourg	SN	Senegal
LAR	Libya	SUD	Sudan
LS	Lesotho	SVC	Vatican
LT	Lithuania	SYR	Syria
LV	Latvia	T	Thailand
M	Malta	TN	Tunisia
MA	Morocco	TR	Turkey
MAL	Malaysia	TT	Trinidad & Tobago
MC	Monaco	UA	Ukraine
MD	Moldova	UAE	United Arab Emirates
MEX	Mexico	USA	United States
MK	Macedonia	WAN	Nigeria
MS	Mauritius	YE	Yemen
MW	Malawi	YU	Yugoslavia
MZ	Mozambique	YV	Venezuela
N	Norway	ZA	South Africa
NA	Netherlands Antilles	ZM	Zambia
NL	Netherlands	ZW	Zimbabwe

CITIES. Correct spellings of some of the cities of the world with populations of more than 2m are listed here. These may be conurbations rather than metropolitan areas. Cities marked [a] are capital cities.

Addis Ababa	*Ethiopia*	Ibadan	*Nigeria*
Ahmadabad	*India*	Istanbul	*Turkey*
Aleppo	*Syria*	Jakarta[a]	*Indonesia*
Alexandria	*Egypt*	Karachi	*Pakistan*
Ankara[a]	*Turkey*	Kiev[a]	*Ukraine*
Athens[a]	*Greece*	Kinshasa[a]	*Congo*
Baghdad[a]	*Iraq*	Lagos	*Nigeria*
Bangalore	*India*	Lahore	*Pakistan*
Bangkok	*Thailand*	Lima[a]	*Peru*
Beijing[a] (Peking)	*China*	Lisbon	*Portugal*
Berlin	*Germany*	London[a]	*UK*
Bogota[a]	*Colombia*	Los Angeles	*USA*
Boston	*USA*	Madrid[a]	*Spain*
Bucharest	*Romania*	Melbourne	*Australia*
Budapest[a]	*Hungary*	Mexico City[a]	*Mexico*
Buenos Aires[a]	*Argentina*	Monterrey	*Mexico*
Cairo[a]	*Egypt*	Montreal	*Canada*
Calcutta	*India*	Moscow[a]	*Russia*
Caracas[a]	*Venezuela*	Mumbai (Bombay)	*India*
Casablanca	*Morocco*	Nagoya	*Japan*
Chengdu	*China*	Nanjing	*China*
Chennai (Madras)	*India*	New York	*USA*
Chicago	*USA*	Osaka	*Japan*
Chongqing	*China*	Paris[a]	*France*
Dallas	*USA*	Philadelphia	*USA*
Damascus[a]	*Syria*	Pusan	*South Korea*
Delhi[a]	*India*	Pyongyang	*North Korea*
Detroit	*USA*	Rio de Janeiro	*Brazil*
Dhaka	*Bangladesh*	Rome[a]	*Italy*
Guadalajara	*Mexico*	St Petersburg	*Russia*
Guangzhou (Canton)	*China*	San Francisco	*USA*
Hanoi[a]	*Vietnam*	Santiago[a]	*Chile*
Harbin	*China*	Santo Domingo[a]	
Havana[a]	*Cuba*		*Dominican Republic*
Ho Chi Minh City		São Paulo	*Brazil*
(Saigon)	*Vietnam*	Seoul[a]	*South Korea*
Hong Kong	*Hong Kong*	Shanghai	*China*
Houston	*USA*	Shenyang	*China*
Hyderabad	*India*	Singapore[a]	*Singapore*

Surabaya	*Indonesia*	Toronto	*Canada*
Sydney	*Australia*	Shanghai	*China*
Taegu	*South Korea*	Washington, DC[a]	*USA*
Taipei[a]	*Taiwan*	Wuhan	*China*
Tashkent[a]	*Uzbekistan*	Xi'an	*China*
Tehran[a]	*Iran*	Yangon[a]	*Myanmar*
Tianjin	*China*	Yokohama	*Japan*
Tokyo[a]	*Japan*		

COMMODITIES AND MANUFACTURED GOODS.

Most countries use the Standard International Trade Classification (sɪᴛᴄ) to describe the goods they import and trade. The classifications are periodically revised: sɪᴛᴄ (3) was introduced in January 1988. A list of the main items follows.

There are 9 sections, giving single digits 1–9; divisions within these sections have 2-digit numbers, and groups within each division have 3-digit numbers. In the list below all sections and divisions are shown together with selected groups. There are also 4-digit sub-groups in the sɪᴛᴄ list, with, for example, 072.3 for "cocoa paste" as a subgroup of 072 ("cocoa"), and further breakdowns for some items into a 5-digit level, with, for example, 072.32 for "cocoa paste, wholly or partly de-fatted". Throughout, nes stands for "not elsewhere specified".

0	Food and live animals
00	Live animals
01	Meat and meat preparations
001	Live animals other than animals of division 03
02	Dairy products and birds' eggs
022	Milk, cream, milk products, excluding butter or cheese
023	Butter and other fats and oils derived from milk
024	Cheese and curd
03	Fish
037	Fish, crustaceans, etc, prepared or preserved
04	Cereals
041	Wheat, including spelt, and meslin, unmilled
042	Rice
043	Barley, unmilled
044	Maize not including sweetcorn, unmilled
05	Vegetables and fruit
057	Fruit and nuts, excluding oil nuts, fresh or dried
06	Sugars and honey
062	Sugar confectionery
07	Coffee, tea, cocoa and spices

071	Coffee and coffee substitutes
072	Cocoa
074	Tea and maté
08	Animal feed
09	Miscellaneous edible products
1	Beverages and tobacco
11	Beverages
112	Alcoholic beverages
12	Tobacco
2	Crude materials, inedible, except fuels
21	Hides, skins and furskins
212	Furskins, raw
22	Oil seeds and oleaginous fruit
23	Crude rubber
24	Cork and wood
245	Fuel wood and wood charcoal, excluding wood waste
25	Pulp and waste paper
26	Textile fibres and waste
263	Cotton textile fibres
266	Synthetic fibres suitable for spinning
268	Wool and other animal hair (including wool tops)
27	Crude fertilisers
273	Stone, sand and gravel
28	Metalliferous ores and metal scrap
281	Iron ore and concentrates
29	Crude animal and vegetable materials
3	Mineral fuels, lubricants and related materials
32	Coal, coke and briquettes
33	Petroleum and petroleum products
333	Crude oil from petroleum or bituminous materials
34	Gas, natural and manufactured
35	Electric current
4	Animal and vegetable oils, fats and waxes
41	Animal oils and fats
42	Fixed vegetable fats and oils
43	Animal fats, vegetable oils and waxes
5	Chemical and related products, nes
51	Organic chemicals

52	Inorganic chemicals
53	Dyeing, tanning and colouring materials
54	Medicinal and pharmaceutical products
55	Oils, perfumes and soaps
554	Soap, cleansing and polishing preparations
56	Fertilisers
57	Plastics in primary forms
58	Plastics in non-primary forms
59	Chemical materials and products

6	Manufactured goods, classified chiefly by material
61	Leather and leather manufactures
62	Rubber manufactures
63	Cork and wood manufactures
64	Paper
65	Textile yarn and fabric
66	Non-metallic mineral manufactures
67	Iron and steel
68	Non-ferrous metals
681	Silver, platinum and other metals of the platinum group
682	Copper
683	Nickel
684	Aluminium
685	Lead
686	Zinc
687	Tin
69	Manufactures of metal

7	Machinery and transport equipment
71	Power generating machinery
713	Internal combustion piston engines, and parts thereof
72	Specialised machinery
721	Agricultural machinery and parts, excluding tractors
724	Textile and leather machinery, and parts thereof
73	Metalworking machinery
74	Industrial machinery
75	Office and automatic data processing (ADP) machines
76	Telecommunications equipment
761	Television receivers
763	Sound recorders, TV recorders, prepared unrecorded media
77	Electrical machinery
78	Road vehicles
781	Motor cars and other motor vehicles

782	Motor vehicles for transport of goods and special purpose motor vehicles
79	Transport equipment
791	Railway vehicles and associated equipment
792	Aircraft and associated equipment, and parts thereof; spacecraft
793	Ships, boats and floating structures

8	Miscellaneous manufactured articles
81	Prefabricated buildings and fixtures
82	Furniture and bedding
83	Travel goods and handbags
831	Trunks, suitcases, vanity cases, briefcases, etc
84	Apparel
841	Men's or boys' coats, jackets, etc, of textile fabrics, not knitted
85	Footwear
87	Professional and scientific instruments
871	Optical instruments and apparatus
88	Photo equipment, watches and clocks
881	Photographic apparatus and equipment
885	Watches and clocks
89	Miscellaneous manufactured goods
895	Office and stationery supplies

9	Commodities and transactions, nes
91	Miscellaneous postal packages
911	Postal packages not classified according to kind
931	Special transactions and commodities not classified according to kind
961	Coin (other than gold coin) not being legal tender
981	Military arms and ammunitions

CURRENCIES.

Country	Currency	Symbol[a]
Afghanistan	afghani	Af
Albania	lek	Lk
Algeria	New (Algerian) dinar	AD
Angola	readjusted kwanza	Kzr
Argentina	peso	Ps
Armenia	dram	Dram
Aruba	Aruban florin	Afl

Country	Currency	Symbol[a]
Australia	Australian dollar	A$
Austria	schilling	ASch
Azerbaijan	manat	Manat
Bahamas	Bahamian dollar	B$
Bahrain	Bahraini dinar	BD
Bangladesh	taka	Tk
Barbados	Barbados dollar	Bds $
Belarus	Belarusian rouble	BRb
Belgium	Belgian franc	Bfr
Belize	Belize dollar	Bz$
Benin	CFA franc	CFAfr
Bermuda	Bermuda dollar	Bda$
Bhutan	ngultrum	Nu
Bolivia	boliviano	Bs
Bosnia & Hercegovina	convertible marka	KM
Botswana	pula	P
Brazil	real	R
Brunei	Brunei dollar/ringgit	Br$
Bulgaria	lev	Lv
Burkina Faso	CFA franc	CFAfr
Burundi	Burundi franc	Bufr
Cambodia	riel	CR
Cameroon	CFA franc	CFAfr
Canada	Canadian dollar	C$
Cape Verde	Cape Verde escudo	CVEsc
Central African Republic	CFA franc	CFAfr
Chad	CFA franc	CFAfr
Chile	Chilean peso	Ps
China	renminbi	Rmb
Colombia	Colombian peso	Ps
Comoros	Comorian franc	Cfr
Congo (Brazzaville)	CFA franc	CFAfr
Congo (Democratic Rep of)	Congolese franc	FC
Costa Rica	Costa Rican colón	C
Côte d'Ivoire	CFA franc	CFAfr
Croatia	kuna	HRK
Cuba	Cuban peso	Ps
Cyprus	Cyprus pound/Turkish lira	C£/TL
Czech Republic	koruna	Kc
Denmark	Danish krone	DKr
Djibouti	Djibouti franc	Dfr

Country	Currency	Symbol[a]
Dominican Republic	Dominican peso	Ps
Dubai	UAE dirham	Dh
Ecuador	sucre	Su
Egypt	Egyptian pound	£E
El Salvador	El Salvador colon	c
Equatorial Guinea	CFA franc	CFAfr
Eritrea	nafka	Nfa
Estonia	kroon	EEK
Ethiopia	birr	Birr
European currency unit	ecu	Ecu
European Union	euro	€
Fiji	Fiji dollar	F$
Finland	markka	FM
France	franc	FFr
Gabon	CFA franc	CFAfr
The Gambia	dalasi	D
Georgia	lari	Lari
Germany	D-mark	DM
Ghana	cedi	C
Greece	drachma	Dr
Grenada	East Caribbean dollar	EC$
Guatemala	quetzal	Q
Guinea	Guinea franc	Gnf
Guinea-Bissau	CFA franc	CFAfr
Guyana	Guyanese dollar	G$
Haiti	gourde	G
Honduras	lempira	La
Hong Kong	Hong Kong dollar	HK$
Hungary	forint	Ft
Iceland	Iceland new króna	Ikr
India	Indian rupee	Rs
Indonesia	rupiah	Rp
Iran	rial	IR
Iraq	Iraqi dinar	ID
Ireland	punt	IR£
Israel	new Israeli shekel	NIS
Italy	lira (pl. lire)	L
Jamaica	Jamaican dollar	J$
Japan	yen	¥
Jordan	Jordan dinar	JD
Kazakhstan	tenge	Tenge

Country	Currency	Symbol[a]
Kenya	Kenya shilling	KSh
Kirgizstan	som	Som
North Korea	North Korean won	Won
South Korea	South Korean won	W
Kuwait	Kuwaiti dinar	KD
Laos	kip	K
Latvia	lat	LVL
Lebanon	Lebanese pound	L£
Lesotho	loti (pl. maloti)	M
Liberia	Liberian dollar	L$
Libya	Libyan dinar	LD
Lithuania	litis	LTL
Luxembourg	Luxembourg franc	Lfr
Macau	pataca	MPtc
Macedonia	Macedonian dinar	Den
Malagasy	Malagasy franc	Mgfr
Malawi	kwacha	MK
Malaysia	Malaysian dollar/ringgit	M$
Mali	CFA franc	CFAfr
Malta	Maltese lira	Lm
Mauritania	ouguiya	UM
Mauritius	Mauritius rupee	MRs
Mexico	Mexican peso	Ps
Moldova	Moldavian leu (pl. lei)	Lei
Mongolia	togrog	Tg
Morocco	dirham	Dh
Mozambique	metical	MT
Myanmar	kyat	Kt
Namibia	Namibia dollar	N$
Nepal	Nepalese rupee	NRs
Netherlands	guilder	G
Netherlands Antilles	Netherlands Antilles guilder	NAG
New Caledonia	French Pacific franc	CFPfr
New Zealand	New Zealand dollar	NZ$
Nicaragua	córdoba	C
Niger	CFA franc	CFAfr
Nigeria	naira	N
Norway	Norwegian krone	NKr
Oman	Omani rial	OR
Pakistan	Pakistan rupee	PRs
Panama	balboa	B

Country	Currency	Symbol[a]
Papua New Guinea	kina	Kina
Paraguay	guarani	G
Peru	nuevo sol	Ns
Philippines	Philippine peso	P
Poland	zloty (pl. zlotys)	Zl
Portugal	escudo	Esc
Puerto Rico	US dollar	$
Qatar	Qatari riyal	QR
Romania	leu (pl. lei)	Lei
Russia	rouble	Rb
Rwanda	Rwandan franc	Rwfr
São Tomé & Príncipe	dobra	Db
Saudi Arabia	Saudi riyal	SR
Senegal	CFA franc	CFAfr
Serbia-Montenegro	Yugoslav dinar	YuD
Seychelles	Seychelles rupee	SRs
Sierra Leone	leone	Le
Singapore	Singapore dollar	S$
Slovakia	Slovak koruna	Kcs
Slovenia	tolar	SIT
Solomon Islands	Solomon Islands dollar	SI$
Somalia	Somali shilling	SoSh
South Africa	rand	R
Spain	peseta	Pta
Sri Lanka	Sri Lanka rupee	SLRs
Sudan	Sudanese pound/dinar	S£/SD
Suriname	Suriname guilder	SG
Swaziland	lilangeni (pl. emalengeni)	E
Sweden	Swedish krona	SKr
Switzerland	Swiss franc	SFr
Syria	Syrian pound	S£
Taiwan	New Taiwan dollar	NT$
Tanzania	Tanzanian shilling	TSh
Thailand	baht	Bt
Togo	CFA franc	CFAfr
Trinidad & Tobago	Trinidad & Tobago dollar	TT$
Tunisia	Tunisian dinar	TD
Turkey	Turkish lira	TL
Turkmenistan	manat	Manat
Uganda	New Ugandan shilling	NUSh
Ukraine	hryvnya	HRN

Country	Currency	Symbol[a]
United Arab Emirates	UAE dirham	Dh
United Kingdom	pound/sterling	£
United States	dollar	$
Uruguay	Uruguayan new peso	Ps
Uzbekistan	som	Som
Vanuatu	vatu	Vt
Venezuela	bolívar	Bs
Vietnam	dong	D
Western Samoa	tala	Tala
Windward & Leeward Islands[b]	East Caribbean dollar	EC$
Yemen	Yemeni rial	YR
Yugoslavia (Serbia-Montenegro)	Yugoslav dinar	YuD
Zambia	kwacha	ZK
Zimbabwe	Zimbabwe dollar	Z$

a See CURRENCIES, page 22, for *The Economist* newspaper usage.

b Antigua & Barbuda, Dominica, Grenada, Monserrat, St Kitts-Nevis, St Lucia, St Vincent & Grenadines, the British Virgin islands.

E

EARTHQUAKES. The Richter scale defines the magnitude of an earthquake in terms of the energy released.

Richter scale		Explosion equivalent	
	Joules	TNT terms	Nuclear terms
0[a]	7.9×10^2	175mg	
1	6.0×10^4	13g	
2	4.0×10^6	0.89kg	
3	2.4×10^8	53kg	
4	1.3×10^{10}	3 tons	
5[b]	6.3×10^{11}	140 tons	
6[c]	2.7×10^{13}	6 kilotons	⅓ atomic bomb
7	1.1×10^{15}	240 kilotons	12 atomic bombs
8	3.7×10^{16}	8.25 megatons	⅓ hydrogen bomb
9	1.1×10^{18}	250 megatons	13 hydrogen bombs
10	3.2×10^{19}	7,000 megatons	350 hydrogen bombs

a About equal to the shock caused by an average man jumping from a table.
b Potentially damaging to structures.
c Potentially capable of general destruction; widespread damage is usually caused above magnitude 6.5.
Note: One atomic bomb is equivalent to 6.3 on the Richter scale, and one hydrogen bomb to 8.2.

Here are some examples.

	Richter scale
San Francisco, 1906	8.3
Chile, 1906	8.6
Gansu, China, 1920	8.6
Kangra, India, 1905	8.6
India/Assam/Tibet, 1950	8.7
Colombia, 1906	8.9
Sanrika, Japan, 1933	8.9
Chile, 1960	9.5
Krakatoa, 1883	9.9 (estimate)

ELEMENTS.

These are the natural and artificially created chemical elements.

Name	Symbol	Name	Symbol
Actinium	Ac	Hydrogen	H
Aluminium	Al	Indium	In
Americium	Am	Iodine	I
Antimony (Stibium)	Sb	Iridium	Ir
Argon	Ar	Iron (Ferrum)	Fe
Arsenic	As	Krypton	Kr
Astatine	At	Lanthanum	La
Barium	Ba	Lawrencium	Lw
Berkelium	Bk	Lead (Plumbum)	Pb
Beryllium	Be	Lithium	Li
Bismuth	Bi	Lutetium	Lu
Boron	B	Magnesium	Mg
Bromine	Br	Manganese	Mn
Cadmium	Cd	Meitnerium	Mt
Calcium	Ca	Mendelevium	Md
Californium	Cf	Mercury (Hydrargyrum)	Hg
Carbon	C	Molybdenum	Mo
Cerium	Ce	Neodymium	Nd
Chlorine	Cl	Neon	Ne
Chromium	Cr	Neptunium	Np
Cobalt	Co	Nickel	Ni
Copper (Cuprum)	Cu	Nielsbohrium	Ns
Curium	Cm	Niobium	Nb
Dysprosium	Dy	Nitrogen	N
Einsteinium	Es	Nobelium	No
Erbium	Er	Osmium	Os
Europium	Eu	Oxygen	O
Fermium	Fm	Palladium	Pd
Fluorine	F	Phosphorus	P
Francium	Fr	Platinum	Pt
Gadolinium	Gd	Plutonium	Pu
Gallium	Ga	Polonium	Po
Germanium	Ge	Potassium (Kalium)	K
Gold (Aurum)	Au	Praseodymium	Pr
Hahnium	Ha	Promethium	Pm
Hassium	Hs	Protactinium	Pa
Helium	He	Radium	Ra
Holmium	Ho	Radon	Rn

Name	Symbol	Name	Symbol
Rhenium	Re	Terbium	Tb
Rhodium	Rh	Thallium	Tl
Rubidium	Rb	Thorium	Th
Ruthenium	Ru	Thulium	Tm
Rutherfordium	Rf	Tin (Stannum)	Sn
Samarium	Sm	Titanium	Ti
Scandium	Sc	Tungsten (Wolfram)	W
Seaborgium	Sg	Unnilhexium	Unh
Selenium	Se	Ununnilium	Uun
Silicon	Si	Uranium	U
Silver (Argentum)	Ag	Vanadium	V
Sodium (Natrium)	Na	Xenon	Xe
Strontium	Sr	Ytterbium	Yb
Sulphur	S	Yttrium	Y
Tantalum	Ta	Zinc	Zn
Technetium	Tc	Zirconium	Zr
Tellurium	Te		

F

FRACTIONS. Do not mingle fractions with decimals. If you need to convert one to the other, use this table. See also FIGURES, pages 27–28.

Fraction	Decimal equivalent
$\frac{1}{2}$	0.5
$\frac{1}{3}$	0.333
$\frac{1}{4}$	0.25
$\frac{1}{5}$	0.2
$\frac{1}{6}$	0.167
$\frac{1}{7}$	0.143
$\frac{1}{8}$	0.125
$\frac{1}{9}$	0.111
$\frac{1}{10}$	0.1
$\frac{1}{11}$	0.091
$\frac{1}{12}$	0.083
$\frac{1}{13}$	0.077
$\frac{1}{14}$	0.071
$\frac{1}{15}$	0.067
$\frac{1}{16}$	0.063
$\frac{1}{17}$	0.059
$\frac{1}{18}$	0.056
$\frac{1}{19}$	0.053
$\frac{1}{20}$	0.05

G

GEOLOGICAL ERAS. Astronomers and geologists give this broad outline of the ages of the universe and the earth.

Era, period and epoch		Years ago m	Characteristics
Origin of the universe (estimates vary markedly)		20,000– 10,000	
Origin of the sun		5,000	
Origin of the earth		4,600	
Pre-Cambrian			
Archean		4,000	First signs of fossilised microbes
Proterozoic		2,500	
Palaeozoic			
Cambrian		570	First appearance of abundant fossils
Ordovician (obsolete)		500	Vertebrates emerge
Silurian		440	Fishes emerge
Devonian		400	Primitive plants emerge
Carboniferous		350	Amphibians emerge
Permian		270	Reptiles emerge
Mesozoic			
Triassic		250	Seed plants emerge
Jurassic		210	Age of dinosaurs
Cretaceous		145	Flowering plants emerge; dinosaurs extinct at end of this period
Cenozoic			
Palaeocene		65	
Tertiary:	Eocene	55	Mammals emerge
	Oligocene	40	
	Miocene	25	
	Pliocene	5	
Quaternary:	Pleistocene	2	Ice ages; stone age man emerges
	Holocene or Recent	10,000[a]	Modern man emerges

a 10,000 years, not 10,000m years.

L

LATIN.
Here are some common Latin words and phrases, together with their translations.

ab initio from the beginning

ad hoc for this object or purpose (implied and "this one only"); therefore, without a system, spontaneously

ad hominem to an individual's interests or passions; used of an argument that takes advantage of the character of the person on the other side

ad infinitum to infinity, that is, endlessly

ad lib. ad libitum, meaning at pleasure. Used adverbially or even as a verb when it means to invent or extemporise

ad valorem according to value (as opposed to volume)

a fortiori with stronger reason

annus mirabilis wonderful year, used to describe a special year, one in which more than one memorable thing has happened; for instance 1666, the year of the Great Fire of London and the English defeats of the Dutch

a priori from cause to effect, that is, deductively or from prior principle

cave "Watch out!" (imperative); once used at boys' schools

caveat emptor let the buyer beware

ceteris paribus other things being equal

cf short for *confer,* meaning compare

circa around or about: used for dates and large quantities; can be abbreviated to **c** or **c.**

de facto in point of fact

de jure from the law; by right

de profundis from the depths

deus ex machina God from a machine; first used of a Greek theatrical convention, where a god would swing on to the stage, high up in a machine, solving humanly insoluble problems and thus resolving the action of a play. Now used to describe a wholly outside person who puts matters right

eg exempli gratia, for example

et al. et alii, and others, used as an abbreviation in bibliographies when citing multiple editorship or authorship to save the writer the bother of writing out all the names. Thus, A. Bloggs *et al., The Occurrence of Endangered Species in the Genus Orthodoptera*

ex cathedra from the chair of office, authoritatively

ex officio   by virtue of one's office, not unofficially

ex parte   from or for one side only

ibid.   ibidem, in the same place; used in footnotes in academic
   works to mean that the quote comes from the same place, book,
   etc

idem   the same, that is mentioned before; like *ibidem*

ie   id est, that is, explains the material immediately in front of it

in absentia   in the absence of, used as "absent"

in camera   in a (private) room, that is, not in public

in re   in the matter of

in situ   in (its) original place

inter alia/inter alios   among other things or people

ipso facto   by that very fact, in the fact itself

loc. cit.   loco citato, in the place cited; used in footnotes to mean
   that the source of the reference or quote has already been given

mea culpa   my fault

mirabile dictu   literally, wonderful to relate

mutatis mutandis   after making the necessary changes

nem. con.   nemine contradicente, no one against; unanimously

op. cit.   opere citato, in the work quoted; similar to *loc. cit.* (q.v.)

pace   despite

pari passu   on the same terms, at an equal pace or rate of progress

passim   adverb, here and there or scattered. Used in indexes to
   indicate that the item is scattered throughout the work and there
   are too many instances to enumerate them all

persona non grata   person not in favour

petitio elenchis   the sin of assuming a conclusion

post eventum   after the event

post hoc, ergo propter hoc   after this, therefore because of this.
   Used fallaciously in argument to show that because something
   comes after something it can be inferred that the first thing
   caused the second thing

post mortem   after death, used as an adjective and also as a noun,
   a clinical examination of a dead body

prima facie   from a first impression, apparently at first sight,
   – no connection with love

primus inter pares   first among equals

pro tem.   pro tempore, for the moment

PS   post scriptum, written afterwards

quid pro quo   something for something (or one thing for
   another), something in return, an equivalent; usually given

q.v.   quod vide, which see; means that the reader should look for
   the word just mentioned (eg in glossary)

re   with regard to, in the matter of

sic   thus; used in brackets in quotes to show writer has made a mistake. "Mrs Thacher (sic) resigned today."

sine die   without (setting) a date

status quo ante   the same state as before; usually shortened to *status quo*. A common usage is "maintaining the status quo"

stet   let it stand or do not delete; cancels an alteration in proofreading; dots are placed under what is to remain

sub judice   under judgment or consideration; not yet decided

sub rosa   under the rose, privately or furtively; not the same as under the gooseberry bush

ultra vires   beyond (one's) legal power

vade mecum   a little book or something carried about on the person; literally "Go with me"

versus   shortened to *v* or *v.*, against; used in legal cases and games

Laws.

Scientific, economic, facetious and fatalistic laws in common use are listed here.

Boyle's Law. The pressure of a gas varies inversely with its volume at constant temperature.

Gresham's Law. When money of a high intrinsic value is in circulation with money of lesser value, it is the inferior currency which tends to remain in circulation, while the other is either hoarded or exported. In other words: "Bad money drives out good".

Grimm's Law. (Concerns mutations of the consonants in the various Germanic languages.) Proto-Indo-European voiced aspirated stops, voiced unaspirated stops and voiceless stops become respectively voiced unaspirated stops, voiceless stops and voiceless fricatives.

Heisenberg's Uncertainty Principle. Energy and time or position and momentum cannot both be accurately measured simultaneously. The product of their uncertainties is h (Planck's constant).

Hooke's Law. The stress imposed on a solid is directly proportional to the strain produced within the elastic limit.

Mendel's Principles. The Law of Segregation is that every somatic cell of an individual carries a pair of hereditary units for each character: the pairs separate during meiosis so that each gamete carries one unit only of each pair.

The Law of Independent Assortment is that the separation of units of each pair is not influenced by that of any other pair.

Murphy's Law. Anything that can go wrong will go wrong.

Ohm's Law. Electric current is directly proportional to electromotive force and inversely proportional to resistance.

Parkinson's Law. First published in *The Economist*, November 19th 1955. The author, C. Northcote Parkinson, sought to expand on the "commonplace observation that work expands so as to fill the time available for its completion". After studying Admiralty staffing levels, he concluded that in any public administrative department not actually at war the staff increase may be expected to follow this formula:

$$x = \frac{2k^m + p}{n}$$

Where k is the number of staff seeking promotion through the appointment of subordinates; p represents the difference between the ages of appointment and retirement; m is the number of hours devoted to answering minutes within the department; and n is the number of effective units being administered. Then x will be the number of new staff required each year.

Mathematicians will, of course, realise that to find the percentage increase they must multiply x by 100 and divide by the total of the previous year, thus:

$$\frac{100\,(2k^m + p)}{yn}\ \%$$

where y represents the total original staff. And this figure will invariably prove to be between 5.17% and 6.56%, irrespective of any variation in the amount of work (if any) to be done.

The Peter Principle. All members of a hierarchy rise to their own level of incompetence.

Say's Law of Markets. A supply of goods generates a demand for the goods.

Laws of Thermodynamics
1. The change in the internal energy of a system equals the sum of the heat added to the system and the work done on it.
2. Heat cannot be transferred from a colder to a hotter body within a system without net changes occurring in other bodies in the system.
3. It is impossible to reduce the temperature of a system to absolute zero in a finite number of steps.

Utz's Laws of Computer Programming. Any given program, when running, is obsolete. If a program is useful, it will have to be changed. Any given program will expand to fill all available memory.

Wolfe's Law of Journalism. You cannot hope/to bribe or twist,/ thank God! the/British journalist./But seeing what/the man will do/ unbribed, there's/no occasion to.

M

Measures

ROUGH CONVERSIONS. For British, American and metric (SI) measures. Metric units not generally recommended as SI units or for use with SI are marked with an asterisk (eg Calorie*).

Acceleration

Standard gravity	=	10 metres per second squared
	=	32 feet per second squared

Area

1 square inch	=	6½ square centimetres
2 square inches	=	13 square centimetres
10¾ square feet	=	1 square metre
43 square feet	=	4 square metres
6 square yards	=	5 square metres
2½ acres	=	1 hectare
5 acres	=	2 hectares
250 acres	=	1 square kilometre
3 square miles	=	8 square kilometres

Density and concentration

4 ounces per UK gallon	=	25 grams per litre
2 ounces per US gallon	=	15 grams per litre
1 pound per cubic foot	=	16 kilograms per cubic metre
62½ pounds per cubic foot	=	1 kilogram per litre
	=	density of 1

Energy

18 British thermal units	=	19 kilojoules
4 British thermal units	=	1 kilocalorie*
1 kilocalorie* ("Calorie"*)	=	4 kilojoules

Force

7¼ poundals	=	1 newton
1 pound-force	=	4½ newtons
1 pounds-force	=	40 newtons
1 kilogram-force	=	10 newtons

Fuel consumption

5 UK gallons per mile	=	14 litres per kilometre
20 miles per UK gallon	=	7 kilometres per litre
20 miles per UK gallon	=	14 litres per 100 kilometres
5 miles per US gallon	=	6 miles per UK gallon

Length

Width of thumb	=	1 inch
	=	25 millimetres
1 inch	=	2½ centimetres
2 inches	=	5 centimetres
1 foot	=	30 centimetres
	=	0.3 metre
3¼ feet	=	1 metre
39 inches	=	1 metre
11 yards	=	10 metres
⅝ mile	=	1 kilometre
5 miles	=	8 kilometres
8 miles	=	7 nautical miles (international)

Power

4 UK horsepower	=	3 kilowatts
72 UK horsepower	=	73 metric horsepower*

Pressure and stress

1 pound-force per square foot	=	48 pascals (newtons per square metre)
1 pound-force per square inch	=	7 kilopascals (kilonewtons per square metre)
1 bar	=	1 standard atmosphere
	=	14½ pounds-force per square inch
100 pounds-force per square inch	=	7 kilograms-force per square centimetre

Velocity (speed)

2 miles per hour	=	3 feet per second
9 miles per hour	=	4 metres per second
8 kilometres per hour	=	5 metres per second
11 kilometres per hour	=	10 feet per second
30 miles per hour	=	48 kilometres per hour
50 miles per hour	=	80 kilometres per hour
70 miles per hour	=	113 kilometres per hour

Volume and capacity

1 teaspoonful	=	5 millilitres
1 UK fluid ounce	=	28 millilitres
26 UK fluid ounces	=	25 US liquid ounces
3 cubic inches	=	49 cubic centimetres
	=	49 millilitres
1¾ UK pints	=	1 litre
7 UK pints	=	4 litres
7 UK quarts	=	8 litres
5 UK pints	=	6 US liquid pints

9 US liquid pints	=	9 litres
1 UK gallon	=	4½ litres
2 UK gallons	=	9 litres
5 UK gallons	=	6 US gallons
1 US gallon	=	3¾ litres
4 US gallons	=	15 litres
3 cubic feet	=	85 cubic decimetres
	=	85 litres
35 cubic feet	=	1 cubic metre
4 cubic yards	=	3 cubic metres
31 UK bushels	=	32 US bushels
27½ UK bushels	=	1 cubic metre
28⅓ US bushels	=	1 cubic metre
11 UK bushels	=	4 hectolitres
14 US bushels	=	5 hectolitres
1 US bushel (heaped)	=	1¼ US bushels (struck)
1 US dry barrel	=	3¼ US bushels
1 US cranberry barrel	=	2¾ bushels
1 barrel (petroleum)	=	42 US gallons
	=	35 UK gallons
1 barrel per day	=	50 tonnes per year

Weight

1 grain	=	65 milligrams
15 grains	=	1 gram
11 ounces	=	10 ounces troy
1 ounce	=	28 grams
1 ounce troy	=	31 grams
1 pound	=	454 grams
35 ounces	=	1 kilogram
2¼ pounds	=	1 kilogram
11 stones	=	70 kilograms
11 US hundredweights	=	5 quintals*
2 UK hundredweights	=	1 quintal*
2,205 pounds	=	1 tonne
11 US tons	=	10 tonnes
62 UK tons	=	63 tonnes
100 UK (long) tons	=	112 US (short) tons

Yield

3 UK or US bushels per acre	=	2 quintals* per hectare
10 UK or US bushels per acre	=	9 hectolitres per hectare
1 UK hundredweight per acre	=	1¼ quintals* per hectare
1 UK ton per acre	=	2½ tonnes per hectare
9 pounds per acre	=	10 kilograms per hectare

Metric system prefixes.

Prefix name & symbol		Factor by which unit is multiplied	Description
atto	a	10^{-18} = 0.000 000 000 000 000 001	
femto	f	10^{-15} = 0.000 000 000 000 001	
pico	p	10^{-12} = 0.000 000 000 001	million millionth; trillionth
nano	n	10^{-9} = 0.000 000 001	thousand millionth; billionth
micro	μ	10^{-6} = 0.000 001	millionth
milli	m	10^{-3} = 0.001	thousandth
centi	c	10^{-2} = 0.01	hundredth
deci	d	10^{-1} = 0.1	tenth
deca (or deka)	da[a]	10^{1} = 10	ten
hecto	h	10^{2} = 100	hundred
kilo	k	10^{3} = 1,000	thousand
myria	my	10^{4} = 10,000	ten thousand
mega	M	10^{6} = 1,000,000	million
giga	G	10^{9} = 1,000,000,000	thousand million; billion
tera	T	10^{12} = 1,000,000,000,000	million million; trillion
peta	P	10^{15} = 1,000,000,000,000,000	
exa	E	10^{18} = 1,000,000,000,000,000,000	

a Sometimes dk is used (eg in Germany).

Units with different equivalents.
Barrel

UK (beer)	= 36 UK gallons
	= 164 litres
USA: dry standard	= 7,056 cubic inches
	= 116 litres
petroleum	= 42 US gallons
	= 159 litres

standard cranberry = 5,826 cubic inches
= 95.5 litres
various (liquid) = 31–42 US gallons
= 117–151 litres

Bushel

UK = 2,219.36 cubic inches
= 36.37 litres
Old English, Winchester ⎤
USA[a] (struck[b]) ⎦ = 2,150 42 cubic inches
= 35.24 litres
USA (heaped[c]) = 2,747 715 cubic inches
= 45.03 litres

a The most usual unit.
b Levelled off at the top.
c Used for apples.

Centner or Zentner

UK = cental of 100 pounds
= 45.36 kilograms
Commercial hundredweight in
several European countries,
generally 50 kilograms = 110.23 pounds
Metric centner of 100 kilograms = 220.46 pounds

Chain

UK: Gunter's/surveyors' = 66 feet
= 20.12 metres}
Engineers' = 100 feet
= 30.48 metres

Foot

UK ⎤
USA customary ⎦ = 12 inches
= 0.304 8 metre
USA survey = 12.000 02 inches
= 0.304 800 6 metre
Canada: Paris foot = 12.789 inches
= 0.325 metre
Cape foot = 12.396 inches
= 0.315 metre
Chinese foot (*che* or *chih*):
old system = 14.1 inches
= 0.358 metre
new system = 13.123 inches
= 0.333 33 metre

Gallon

UK	= 277.42 cubic inches
	= 4.546 litres

Old English, Winchester, Wine ⎱
  USA, liquid ⎰ = 231 cubic inches
  = 3.785 litres
  USA, dry = 268.802 5 cubic inches
  = 0.004 4 cubic metre

Gill

UK	= 8.669 cubic inches
	= 142.1 millilitres
USA	= 7.218 75 cubic inches
	= 118.3 millilitres

Hundredweight

UK ⎱
USA, long ⎰ = 112 pounds
  = 50.8 kilograms
  USA, short = 100 pounds
  = 45.4 kilograms

Link

UK: Gunter's/surveyors' = 0.66 foot
  = 0.201 2 metre
  Engineers' = 1 foot
  = 0.304 8 metre

Mile

UK: imperial = 5,280 feet
  = 1.609 344 kilometres
  geographical ⎱ = 6,080 feet
  = 1.853 184 kilometres[a]
  nautical ⎰
  sea
  USA = 5,280 feet
  = 1.609 344 kilometres
  International nautical = 1,852 metres
  = 6,076.12 feet

a In practice sometimes 6,000 feet = 1.8288 kilometres

Ounce

Dry: ounce = 437½ grains
  = 28.35 grams
  ounce troy = 480 grains
  = 31.01 grams
  Liquid[a] or fluid[b] ounce: UK = 1.734 cubic inches
  = 28.4 millilitres

| | USA | = | 1.805 cubic inches |
| | | = | 29.6 millilitres |

a 16 liquid ounces = 1 liquid pint
b 20 fluid ounces = 1 pint

Peck

	UK	=	554.839 cubic inches
		=	9.092 cubic decimetres (litres)
	USA	=	537.605 cubic inches
		=	8.810 cubic decimetres (litres)

Pint

	UK	=	34.677 4 cubic inches
		=	0.568 litre
	USA: dry	=	33.600 312 5 cubic inches
		=	0.551 cubic decimetre (litre)
	liquid	=	28.875 cubic inches
		=	0.473 litre

Pound

UK ⎫
USA ⎰ avoirdupois pound = 0.454 kilogram

USA: troy pound	=	0.373 kilogram
	=	0.823 pound (avoirdupois)
Spanish (libra)	=	0.460 kilogram
	=	1.014 pounds (avoirdupois)
"Amsterdam"	=	0.494 kilogram
	=	1.089 pounds (avoirdupois)
Danish (pund)	=	0.5 kilogram
	=	1.102 pounds (avoirdupois)
Française (livre)	=	0.490 kilogram
	=	1.079 pounds (avoirdupois)

Quart

	UK	=	69.355 cubic inches
		=	1.137 litres
	USA: dry	=	67.200 625 cubic inches
		=	1.101 cubic decimetres (litres)
	liquid	=	57.75 cubic inches
		=	0.946 litre

Quarter

	UK: capacity	=	8 bushels
		=	64 gallons
		=	2.909 hectolitres
		=	0.290 9 cubic metre
	weight (mass)	=	28 pounds
		=	12.701 kilograms

cloth	=	9 inches
	=	22.86 centimetres
wines and spirits	=	27½–30 gallons
	=	125–136 litres

Quintal

Hundredweight: UK	=	112 pounds
	=	50.8 kilograms
USA	=	100 pounds
	=	45.4 kilograms
Metric quintal	=	100 kilograms
	=	220.46 pounds
Spanish quintal	=	46 kilograms
	=	101.4 pounds

Stone

UK: Imperial	=	14 pounds
	=	6.350 kilograms
Smithfield	=	8 pounds
	=	3.629 kilograms

Ton

UK: weight (mass)	=	2,240 pounds
	=	1.016 tonnes
shipping: register	=	100 cubic feet
	=	2.832 cubic metres
USA: short	=	2,000 pounds
	=	0.907 tonne
long	=	2,240 pounds
	=	1.016 tonnes
Metric ton (tonne)	=	1,000 kilograms
	=	2,204.62 pounds
Spanish: short (corta)	=	2,000 libras
	=	0.920 2 tonne
	=	2,028.7 pounds
long (larga)	=	2,240 libras
	=	1.030 6 tonnes
	=	2,272.1 pounds

See also MEASUREMENTS, page 40.

N

NATIONAL ACCOUNTS.
These are the definitions adopted by the United Nations in 1968 but national accounts now refer to gross national product as gross national income (GNI).

Final expenditure
= private final consumption expenditure ("consumers' expenditure")
+ government final consumption expenditure
+ increase in stocks
+ gross fixed capital formation
+ exports of goods and services

Gross domestic product (GDP) at market prices
= final expenditure
− imports of goods and services

Gross national income or product (GNI/GNP) at market prices
= gross domestic product at market prices
+ net property income from other countries

Gross domestic product at factor cost
= gross domestic product at market prices
− indirect taxes
+ subsidies

O

Olympic games.

I	Athens	1896	XIV	London	1948
II	Paris	1900	XV	Helsinki	1952
III	St Louis	1904	XVI	Melbourne	1956
	Athens	1906	XVII	Rome	1960
IV	London	1908	XVIII	Tokyo	1964
V	Stockholm	1912	XIX	Mexico City	1968
VI	Berlin (cancelled)	1916	XX	Munich	1972
VII	Antwerp	1920	XXI	Montreal	1976
VIII	Paris	1924	XXII	Moscow	1980
IX	Amsterdam	1928	XXIII	Los Angeles	1984
X	Los Angeles	1932	XXIV	Seoul	1988
XI	Berlin	1936	XXV	Barcelona	1992
XII	Tokyo/Helsinki (cancelled)	1940	XXVI	Atlanta	1996
			XXVII	Sydney	2000
XIII	London (cancelled)	1944	XXVIII	Athens	2004

Organisations

These are the exact names and abbreviated titles of the main international organisations. Where membership is small or exclusive, members are listed too.

Asean. Association of South East Asian Nations.
Members

Brunei	Malaysia	Singapore
Cambodia[a]	Myanmar	Thailand
Indonesia	Papua New Guinea[a]	Vietnam
Laos	Philippines	

a Observer status.

Bis. Bank for International Settlements. The central bankers' central bank, in Basle.
Members

Argentina	Bosnia[a]
Australia	Brazil
Austria	Bulgaria
Belgium	Canada

China
Croatia[a]
Czech Republic
Denmark
Estonia
European Central Bank
Finland
France
Germany
Greece
Hong Kong
Hungary
Iceland
India
Indonesia
Ireland
Italy
Japan
Latvia
Lithuania
Macedonia[a]

Malaysia
Mexico
Netherlands
Norway
Poland
Portugal
Romania
Russia
Saudi Arabia
Singapore
Slovakia
Slovenia[a]
South Africa
South Korea
Spain
Sweden
Switzerland
Thailand
Turkey
United Kingdom
United States

a Pending.

CARICOM. Caribbean Community and Common Market.
Members

Antigua and Barbuda
Bahamas
Barbados
Belize
British Virgin Islands[a]
Dominica
Grenada
Guyana
Haiti

Jamaica
Montserrat
St Kitts-Nevis
St Lucia
St Vincent and the Grenadines
Suriname
Trinidad and Tobago
Turks and Caicos Islands[a]

a Associate members.

COMMONWEALTH.
Members

Antigua and Barbuda
Australia
Bahamas
Bangladesh
Barbados

Belize
Botswana
Brunei
Cameroon
Canada

Cyprus
Dominica
Fiji Islands
The Gambia
Ghana
Grenada
Guyana
India
Jamaica
Kenya
Kiribati
Lesotho
Malawi
Malaysia
Maldives
Malta
Mauritius
Mozambique
Namibia
Nauru
New Zealand
Nigeria[a]

Pakistan[b]
Papua New Guinea
St Kitts-Nevis
St Lucia
St Vincent and the Grenadines
Samoa
Seychelles
Sierra Leone
Singapore
Solomon Islands
South Africa[c]
Sri Lanka
Swaziland
Tanzania
Tonga
Trinidad and Tobago
Tuvalu
Uganda
United Kingdom
Vanuatu
Zambia
Zimbabwe

a Membership suspended in November 1995, but renewed in late 1999.
b Pakistan was suspended in late 1999.
c South Africa withdrew in 1961, but rejoined in 1994.

Dependencies and associated states
Australia:

Ashmore and Cartier Islands
Australian Antarctic
Christmas Island
Cocos (Keeling) Islands

Coral Sea Islands
Heard and McDonald Islands
Norfolk Island

New Zealand:

Cook Islands
Niue

Ross Dependency
Tokelau Islands

United Kingdom:

Anguilla
Ascension,
  Tristan da Cunha
Bermuda
British Antarctic Territory
British Indian Ocean Territory
British Virgin Islands

Cayman Islands
Falkland Islands
Gibraltar
Guernsey and Jersey
Isle of Man
Montserrat
Pitcairn Islands

South Georgia and   St Helena and dependencies
  South Sandwich Islands   Ascension, Tristan da Cunha
                          Turks and Caicos Islands

COMMONWEALTH OF INDEPENDENT STATES (CIS). Founded in December 1991 by the former Soviet Socialist Republics.
Members

Armenia	Kazakhstan	Tajikistan
Azerbaijan	Kirgizstan	Turkmenistan
Belarus	Moldova	Ukraine
Georgia	Russia	Uzbekistan

EU. European Union, the collective designation of three organisations with common membership. These organisations are: the European Coal and Steel Community (ECSC), European Economic Community (EEC) and European Atomic Energy Community (EURATOM). They merged to become the European Community (EC) in 1967. In November 1993 when the Maastricht treaty came into force the EC was incorporated into the European Union. Founding members are marked [a].
Members

Austria	Germany[a]	Netherlands[a]
Belgium[a]	Greece	Portugal
Denmark	Ireland	Spain
Finland	Italy[a]	Sweden
France[a]	Luxembourg[a]	United Kingdom

ECOWAS. Economic Community of West African States.
Members

Benin	Guinea	Niger
Burkina Faso	Guinea-Bissau	Nigeria
Cape Verde	Liberia	Senegal
Côte d'Ivoire	Mali	Sierra Leone
The Gambia	Mauritania	Togo
Ghana		

EFTA. European Free Trade Association.
Members

Iceland	Norway
Liechtenstein	Switzerland

FRANC ZONE. Comité Monétaire de la Zone Franc.
Members

Benin	Burkina Faso[a]	Cameroon[b]

Central African	Côte d'Ivoire[a]	Niger
Republic[b]	Equatorial Guinea[b]	Senegal[a]
Chad[b]	France[c]	Togo[a]
Comoros[b]	Gabon[b]	
Congo, Democratic	Guinea-Bissau	
Republic of[b]	Mali[a]	

a Member of Banque Centrale des Etats de l'Afrique de l'Ouest.

b Member of Banque des Etats de l'Afrique Centrale.

c Metropolitan France, Mayotte, St Pierre and Miquelon and the Overseas Departments and Territories.

GCC. Co-operation Council for the Arab States of the Gulf. Its normal shorthand name is Gulf Co-operation Council.

Members

Bahrain	Qatar
Kuwait	Saudi Arabia
Oman	United Arab Emirates

GROUP OF SEVEN (G7). A subset of the G10, whose members are Canada, France, Germany, Italy, Japan, the UK and the USA. It has no organisational structure. Holds formal summit meetings of heads of state or their representatives. Although primarily a forum for discussing economic problems, the G7 is increasingly becoming involved in politics.

GROUP OF EIGHT (G8). G7 plus Russia.

GROUP OF TEN (G10). The countries – Belgium, Canada, France, Germany, Italy, Japan, the Netherlands, Sweden, Switzerland, the UK and the USA – that agreed to provide credit of $6 billion to the International Monetary Fund in 1962, known as the General Arrangement to Borrow. The G10 is a convenient forum for discussing international monetary arrangements; it hatched the Smithsonian agreement and currency changes in 1971. The G10 also meets through its central bank, the Bank for International Settlements (BIS) based in Basle.

IATA. International Air Transport Association. Head offices: Montreal, Geneva and Singapore. *Members*: most international airlines.

LAIA (ALADI). Latin American Integration Association.

Members

Argentina	Brazil	Colombia[a]
Bolivia[a]	Chile	Cuba[b]

Ecuador[a]	Paraguay	Venezuela[a]
Mexico	Peru[a]	
Panama	Uruguay	

a These countries are also members of the Andean Group.
b Subject to receipt of instrument of ratification.

NATO. North Atlantic Treaty Organisation.

Members

Belgium	Greece	Poland
Canada	Iceland	Portugal
Czech Republic	Italy	Spain
Denmark	Luxembourg	Turkey
France[a]	Netherlands	United Kingdom
Germany	Norway	United States
Hungary		

a France withdrew from the integrated military command structure.

NATO's "Partnership for Peace" (PfP) programme, launched in 1994, is aimed at getting former communist countries in Eastern Europe, the Nordic countries and Austria, and the former Soviet Union to take part in a range of military co-operation arrangements without having the full obligations or benefits of NATO membership. In 1998 NATO had 27 PfP partners.

OAU. Organization of African Unity.

Members

Algeria	Egypt	Mauritius
Angola	Equatorial Guinea[a]	Mozambique
Benin	Eritrea	Namibia
Botswana	Ethiopia	Niger
Burkina Faso	Gabon	Nigeria
Burundi	The Gambia	Rwanda
Cameroon	Ghana	São Tomé and
Cape Verde	Guinea	Principe[a]
Central African	Guinea-Bissau[a]	Senegal
Republic[a]	Kenya	Seychelles[a]
Chad[a]	Lesotho	Sierra Leone[a]
Comoros[a]	Liberia	Somalia
Congo (Brazzaville)	Libya	South Africa
Côte d'Ivoire	Madagascar	Sudan
Democratic Republic	Malawi	Swaziland
of Congo	Mali	Tanzania
Djibouti	Mauritania	Togo

Tunisia Zambia
Uganda Zimbabwe
a Suspended in 1995 for non-payment of dues.

The Sahara Arab Democratic Republic (Western Sahara) was admitted in February 1982, following recognition by 26 of the 50 members. Its membership was disputed by Morocco and others which claimed that a two-thirds majority was needed to admit a state whose existence is in question. Morocco withdrew from the OAU with effect from November 1985.

OAS. Organization of American States. Has many permanent non-member observers.
Members

Antigua and	Dominica	Panama
Barbuda	Dominican	Paraguay
Argentina	Republic	Peru
Bahamas	Ecuador	St Kitts-Nevis
Barbados	El Salvador	St Lucia
Belize	Grenada	St Vincent and the
Bolivia	Guatemala	Grenadines
Brazil	Guyana	Suriname
Canada	Haiti	Trinidad and
Chile	Honduras	Tobago
Colombia	Jamaica	United States
Costa Rica	Mexico	Uruguay
Cuba[a]	Nicaragua	Venezuela

a Suspended in 1962.

OECD. Organisation for Economic Co-operation and Development. Capitalism's club, based in Paris.
Members

Australia	Hungary	Poland
Austria	Iceland	Portugal
Belgium	Ireland	South Korea
Canada	Italy	Spain
Czech Republic	Japan	Sweden
Denmark	Luxembourg	Switzerland
Finland	Mexico	Turkey
France	Netherlands	United Kingdom
Germany	New Zealand	United States
Greece	Norway	

Slovakia has participated in the OECD's "Partners in transition" programme since 1991. An agreement was signed with Russia in June 1994.

OPEC. Organization of Petroleum Exporting Countries.

Members

Algeria	Iraq	Qatar
Gabon[a]	Kuwait	Saudi Arabia
Indonesia	Libya	United Arab Emirates
Iran	Nigeria	Venezuela

a Withdrew in 1996.

OSCE. Organization for Security and Co-operation in Europe. Originally founded in 1975 as CSCE (Conference on Security and Co-operation in Europe). 55 members.

THE UNITED NATIONS. New York.

General Assembly	Trusteeship Council
Security Council	International Court of Justice
Economic and Social Council (ECOSOC)	

Main bodies

Regional Commissions of ECOSOC		*Head office*
Economic Commission for Africa	ECA	Addis Ababa
Economic Commission for Europe	ECE	Geneva
Economic and Social Commission for Asia and the Pacific	ESCAP	Bangkok
Economic Commission for Latin America and the Caribbean	ECLAC	Santiago, Chile
Economic and Social Commission for Western Asia	ESCWA	Amman

Other United Nations bodies

Office of the United Nations Emergency Relief Co-ordinator	UNDRO	Geneva
United Nations Centre for Human Settlements	Habitat	Nairobi
United Nations Children's Fund	UNICEF	New York
United Nations Conference on Trade and Development	UNCTAD	Geneva
United Nations Development Programme	UNDP	New York
United Nations Environment Programme	UNEP	Nairobi
United Nations High Commissioner for Refugees	UNHCR	Geneva

United Nations International Drug Control Programme	UNDCP	Vienna
United Nations Observer Missions and Peace-keeping Forces		New York
United Nations Population Fund	UNFPA	New York
United Nations Relief and Works Agency for Palestine Refugees in the Near East	UNRWA	Vienna
World Food Council	WFC	Rome
World Food Programme	WFP	Rome

Specialised agencies within the UN system

Food and Agriculture Organization	FAO	Rome
International Bank for Reconstruction and Development (World Bank)	IBRD	Washington, DC
International Bureau of Education	IBE	Geneva
International Centre for Settlement of Investment Disputes	ICSID	Washington, DC
International Civil Aviation Organization	ICAO	Montreal
International Development Association	IDA	Washington, DC
International Finance Corporation	IFC	Washington, DC
International Fund for Agricultural Development	IFAD	Rome
International Labour Organisation	ILO	Geneva
International Maritime Organization	IMO	London
International Monetary Fund	IMF	Washington, DC
International Telecommunications Union	ITU	Geneva
Multilateral Investment Guarantee Agency	MIGA	Washington, DC
United Nations Educational, Scientific and Cultural Organization	UNESCO	Paris
United Nations Industrial Development Organization	UNIDO	Vienna
Universal Postal Union	UPU	Berne
World Health Organization	WHO	Geneva
World Intellectual Property Organization	WIPO	Geneva
World Meteorological Organization	WMO	Geneva

Other organs related to the UN

International Atomic Energy Agency	IAEA	Vienna
International Sea-Bed Authority		Kingston, Jamaica
World Trade Organization	WTO	Geneva

R

ROMAN NUMERALS.

I	1	XIV	14	CC	200
II	2	XV	15	D	500
III	3	XVI	16	DCC	700
IV	4	XVII	17	DCCXIX	719
V	5	XVIII	18	CM	900
VI	6	XIX	19	M	1000
VII	7	XX	20	MC	1100
VIII	8	XXI	21	MCX	1110
IX	9	XXX	30	MCMXCI	1991
X	10	XL	40	MM	2000
XI	11	L	50	MMX	2010
XII	12	XC	90		
XIII	13	C	100		

S

STATES, REGIONS, PROVINCES, COUNTIES AND LOCAL AUTHORITIES

Here are the correct spellings of the main administrative subdivisions of industrialised countries. Accents should be used. See also COUNTRIES AND THEIR INHABITANTS.

AUSTRALIA (Commonwealth of Australia)

States	*Territories*
New South Wales	Australian Capital Territory
Queensland	Northern Territory
South Australia	
Tasmania	
Victoria	
Western Australia	

BELGIUM (Kingdom of Belgium)

Provinces

Antwerp (Anvers)	Limbourg
Brabant	Luxembourg
East Flanders	Namur
Hainaut	West Flanders
Liège	

BRAZIL (Federal Republic of Brazil)

States

Acre	Pernambuco
Alagoas	Piauí
Amapá	Rio de Janeiro
Amazonas	Rio Grande do Norte
Bahia	Rio Grande do Sul
Ceará	Rondônia
Espírito Santo	Roraima
Goiás	Santa Catarina
Maranhão	São Paulo
Mato Grosso	Sergipe
Mato Grosso do Sul	Tocantins
Minas Gerais	Distrito Federal
Paraíba	(Federal District, Brasília)
Parana	

CANADA
Provinces

Alberta	Prince Edward Island
British Columbia	Quebec (Québec)
Manitoba	Saskatchewan
New Brunswick	
Newfoundland	*Territories*
Nova Scotia	Northwest Territories
Ontario	Nunavut
	Yukon Territory

FRANCE (Republic of France)
Regions

Alsace	Ile-de-France
Aquitaine	Languedoc-Roussillon
Auvergne	Limousin
Basse-Normandie	Lorraine
Brittany (Bretagne)	Midi-Pyrénées
Burgundy (Bourgogne)	Nord Pas-de-Calais
Centre	Pays de la Loire
Champagne-Ardenne	Picardy (Picardie)
Corsica (Corse)	Poitou-Charentes
Franche-Comté	Provence-Alpes-Côte d'Azur
Haute-Normandie	Rhône-Alpes

GERMANY (Federal Republic of Germany)
States (in German *Länder*)

Baden-Württemberg	North Rhine-Westphalia
Bavaria (Bayern)	(Nordrhein-Westfalen)
Berlina	Rhineland-Palatinate
Brandenburgb	(Rheinland-Pfalz)
Bremen	Saarland
Hamburg	Saxony (Sachsen)b
Hesse (Hessen)	Saxony-Anhalt (Sachsen-
Lower Saxony (Niedersachsen)	Anhalt)b
Thuringia (Thüringen)b	Schleswig-Holstein
Mecklenburg-West Pomerania	Thuringiab
(Vorpommern)b	

a Formerly West Berlin.
b Former East German states.

IRELAND (Republic of Ireland)

Provinces	Counties	
Connacht	Galway	Mayo
	Galway County Borough	Roscommon
	Leitrim	Sligo
Leinster	Carlow	Louth
	Dublin County Borough	Meath
	Dun Laoghaire-Rathdown	Offaly
	Fingal	South Dublin
	Kildare	Westmeath
	Kilkenny	Wexford
	Laoighis	Wicklow
	Longford	
Munster	Clare	Limerick County Borough
	Cork	
	Cork County Borough	Tipperary
	Kerry	Waterford
	Limerick	Waterford County Borough
Ulster	Cavan	Monaghan
	Donegal	

ITALY (Italian Republic)

Regions

Abruzzi
Basilicata
Calabria
Campania
Emilia-Romagna
Friuli-Venezia Giulia
Lazio
Liguria
Lombardy (Lombardia)
Marche

Molise
Piedmont (Piemonte)
Puglia
Sardinia (Sardegna)
Sicily (Sicilia)
Tuscany (Toscana)
Trentino-Alto Adige
Umbria
Valle d'Aosta
Veneto

NETHERLANDS (Kingdom of the Netherlands)

Provinces

Drenthe
Flevoland
Friesland
Gelderland
Groningen
Limburg

Noord-Brabant
Noord-Holland
Overijssel
Utrecht
Zeeland
Zuid-Holland

Russia

There are 89 members (federal territorial units) of the Russian Federation. Since 1993 these members consist of 21 autonomous republics, six *krais* (provinces), 49 *oblasts* (regions), two cities of federal status (Moscow and St Petersburg), one autonomous *oblast* (the Jewish Autonomous Area) and ten autonomous *krugs* (districts). Each unit is grouped into one of 11 Economic Areas.

Economic Areas

Central	Far Eastern (or	Urals
Central Chernozem	Pacific)	Volga
(Black Earth)	North Caucasus	Volga-Vyatka
Eastern Siberian	North-Western	Western Siberian
	Northern	

Autonomous Republics

Adygega	Kabardino-Balkaria	Mari-El
Altai	Republic	Mordovian Republic
Bashkortostan	Kalmykia	North Ossetian
Buryatia	Karachevo-Cherkess	Republic
Chechnya	Republic	Sakha (Yakutia)
Chuvashia	Karelia	Tatarstan
Dagestan	Khakasia	Tuva
Ingush Republic	Komi	Udmur Republic

Krais

Altai	Krasnodar	Maritime
Khabarovsk	Krasnoyarsk	Stavropol

Autonomous Krugs

Agin-Buryat	Komi-Permyak	Ust-Orda Buryat
Chukchi	Koriak	Yamat Nenets
Evenk	Nenets	
Khanty-Mansy	Taimyr	

Spain

Autonomous Communities

Andalusia	Basque Country	Castilla y León
Aragón	(Euskadi)	Catalonia (Cataluña)
Asturias	Canary Islands	Ceuta[a]
Balearic Islands	(Canarias)	Extremadura
(Baleares)	Cantabria	Galicia
	Castilla-La Mancha	Madrid

Melilla[a]   Rioja, La
Murcia   Valencian
Navarra   Community

UNITED KINGDOM
England: Unitary Councils

Barnsley
Bath and North-east
   Somerset
Birmingham
Blackburn with
   Darwen
Blackpool
Bolton
Bournemouth
Bracknell Forest
Bradford
Brighton and Hove
Bristol
Bury
Calderdale
Coventry
Darlington
Derby
Doncaster
Dudley
East Riding of
   Yorkshire
Gateshead
Halton
Hartlepool
Herefordshire
Isle of Wight
Kingston upon Hull
Kirklees
Knowsley

Leeds
Leicester
Liverpool
Luton
Manchester
Medway
Middlesborough
Milton Keynes
Newcastle upon Tyne
North-east
   Lincolnshire
North Lincolnshire
North Somerset
North Tyneside
Nottingham
Oldham
Peterborough
Plymouth
Poole
Portsmouth
Reading
Redcar and
   Cleveland
Rochdale
Rotherham
Rutland
St Helens
Salford
Sandwell
Sefton

Sheffield
Slough
Solihull
South Gloucestershire
Southampton
Southend
South Tyneside
Stockport
Stockton-on-Tees
Stoke-on-Trent
Sunderland
Swindon
Tameside
Telford and Wrekin
Thurrock
Torbay
Trafford
Wakefield
Walsall
Warrington
West Berkshire
Wigan
Windsor and
   Maidenhead
Wirral
Wokingham
Wolverhampton
York

England: County Councils

Bedfordshire
Buckinghamshire
Cambridgeshire
Cheshire
Cornwall

Cumbria
Derbyshire
Devon
Dorset
Durham

East Sussex
Essex
Gloucestershire
Hampshire
Hertfordshire

Kent
Lancashire
Leicestershire
Lincolnshire
Norfolk
Northamptonshire
Northumberland

North Yorkshire
Nottinghamshire
Oxfordshire
Shropshire
Somerset
Staffordshire
Suffolk

Surrey
Warwickshire
West Sussex
Wiltshire
Worcestershire

Wales: Unitary Authorities

Blaenau Gwent
Bridgend
Caerphilly
Cardiff
Carmarthenshire
Ceredigion
Conwy
Denbighshire

Flintshire
Gwynedd
Isle of Anglesey
Merthyr Tydfil
Monmouthshire
Neath Port Talbot
Newport
Pembrokeshire

Powys
Rhondda Cynon Taff
Swansea
Torfaen
Vale of Glamorgan
Wrexham

Scotland: Authorities

Aberdeen City
Aberdeenshire
Angus
Argyll and Bute
Clackmannanshire
Dumfries and
   Galloway
Dundee City
East Ayrshire
East Dunbartonshire
East Lothian
East Renfrewshire

Edinburgh, City of
Eilean Siar/Western
   Isles
Falkirk
Fife
Glasgow City
Highland
Inverclyde
Midlothian
Moray
North Ayrshire
North Lanarkshire

Orkney Islands
Perth and Kinross
Renfrewshire
Scottish Borders
Shetland Islands
South Ayrshire
South Lanarkshire
Stirling
West Dunbartonshire
West Lothian

Northern Ireland: District Councils

Antrim
Ards
Armagh
Ballymena
Ballymoney
Banbridge
Belfast
Carrickfergus
Castlereagh

Coleraine
Cookstown
Craigavon
Derry
Down
Dungannon
Fermanagh
Larne
Limavady

Lisburn
Magherafelt
Moyle
Newry and Mourne
Newtownabbey
North Down
Omagh
Strabane

Northern Ireland: *Counties*

Antrim	Down	Londonderry City
Armagh	Fermanagh	Tyrone
Belfast City	Londonderry	

UNITED STATES

States

Alabama	Kentucky	Ohio
Alaska	Louisiana	Oklahoma
Arizona	Maine	Oregon
Arkansas	Maryland	Pennsylvania
California	Massachusetts	Rhode Island
Colorado	Michigan	South Carolina
Connecticut	Minnesota	South Dakota
Delaware	Mississippi	Tennessee
Federal District of	Missouri	Texas
Columbia (DC)[a]	Montana	Utah
Florida	Nebraska	Vermont
Georgia	Nevada	Virginia
Hawaii	New Hampshire	Washington
Idaho	New Jersey	West Virginia
Illinois	New Mexico	Wisconsin
Indiana	New York	Wyoming
Iowa	North Carolina	
Kansas	North Dakota	

a DC is not a state.

Stockmarket indices

January 2000. These lists are frequently changed.

THE FINANCIAL TIMES STOCK EXCHANGE 100 SHARE INDEX. Consists of the following.

3i Group	AstraZeneca
Abbey National	BAA
Alliance & Leicester	Bank of Scotland (Governor &
Allied Domecq	Co. of)
Allied Zurich	Barclays
AMVESCAP	Bass
Anglo American	BG Group
ARM Holdings	Billiton
Associated British Foods	Blue Circle Industries

BOC Group
Boots Co.
BP Amoco
British Aerospace
British Airways
British American Tobacco
British Sky Broadcasting Group
British Telecommunications
Cable & Wireless
Cadbury Schweppes
Carlton Communications
Centrica
CGU
COLT Telecom Group
Compass Group
Corus Group
Daily Mail & General Trust
Diageo
Dixons Group
EMI Group
Energis Group
Gallaher
GKN
Glaxo Wellcome
Granada Group
Great Universal Stores
Halifax Group
Hanson
Hays
Hilton
HSBC Holdings
Imperial Chemical Industries
Imperial Tobacco Group
Invensys
Kingfisher
Land Securities
Legal & General Group
Lloyds TSB Group
Logica
Marconi
Marks and Spencer
Misys
National Grid Group (The)

National Power
National Westminster Bank
Norwich Union
Old Mutual
Pearson
Peninsular and Oriental Steam
  Navigation Company
PowerGen
Prudential
Railtrack Group
Reckitt Benckiser
Reed International
Rentokil Initial
Reuters Group
Rio Tinto
Rolls-Royce
Royal & Sun Alliance Insurance
  Group
Royal Bank of Scotland Group
  (The)
Sage Group (The)
Sainsbury (J)
Schroders
Scottish & Newcastle
Scottish & Southern Energy
Scottish Power
Sema Group
Severn Trent
Shell Transport and Trading Co.
SmithKline Beecham
South African Breweries
Standard Chartered
Sun Life and Provincial Holdings
Telewest Communications
Tesco
Thames Water
Unilever
United News & Media
United Utilities
Vodafone Airtouch
Whitbread
Wolseley
Woolwich
WPP Group

THE DOW JONES INDUSTRIAL AVERAGE consists of these companies.

ALCOA Inc.
American Express Co.
AT&T Corp.
Boeing Co.
Caterpillar Inc.
Citigroup Inc.
Coca-Cola Co.
DuPont
Eastman Kodak Co.
Exxon Mobil Corp.
General Electric Co.
General Motors Corp.
Hewlett-Packard Co.
Home Depot Inc.
Honeywell International Inc.
International Business
    Machines Corp.

International Paper Co.
Intel Corp.
Johnson & Johnson
McDonald's Corp.
Merck & Co.
Microsoft Corp.
Minnesota Mining &
    Manufacturing Co.
J.P. Morgan & Co.
Philip Morris Cos.
Procter & Gamble Co.
SBC Communications Inc.
United Technologies Corp.
Wal-Mart Stores Inc.
Walt Disney Co.